Women and Politics Worldwide

Women and Politics Worldwide

A K Yadav

MD PUBLICATIONS PVT LTD
NEW DELHI
www.mdppl.com

Published by :

MD Publications Pvt Ltd
"MD House", 11, Darya Ganj,
New Delhi-110 002
Phone : +91-11-45355555
E-mail : contact@mdppl.com
Website : www.mdppl.com

ISBN : 978-81-7533-293-5

Published and Printed by Mr. Pranav Gupta on behalf of
MD Publications Pvt Ltd at Printext, New Delhi.

PREFACE

Women in politics have historically been underrepresented in Western societies compared to men. Many women, however, have been politically elected to be heads of state and government. Most prominent may be the female leaders of world powers such as Prime Minister of the United Kingdom Margaret Thatcher, Prime Minister of India Indira Gandhi, Prime Minister of Israel Golda Meir, Chancellor of Germany Angela Merkel, Prime Minister of Canada Kim Campbell, Prime Minister of France Edith Cresson, President of the People's Republic of China Soong Ching-ling (AKA Rosamond Soong), and Director of the Cultural Revolution, dictator Jiang Qing.

Since women make up more than 50 percent of the total population, one standard might be that women should hold half the elected positions, but obviously there is no agreement on what is the right number or the number that might indicate progress in achieving better representation. In discussing numbers of women in office, the question arises about why we should care that more women serve in elected positions. Three ways of answering that question are: it is fair; society needs their talents; and, they make a difference.

The matter of fairness becomes particularly important when addressing the barriers to women achieving elective office and raises the questions of why they are not included in an affirmative manner. As for talent, this concept, which encompasses knowledge and experience, recognizes that women have a demonstrated track record of educational achievement, and leadership in political and civic affairs that is useful to society and therefore should not be ignored.

Given all the efforts women have organized to attain political office and the evidence they have marshaled that women's involvement makes a difference, why doesn't it happen? The reasons are probably imbedded in our political structure. The strength of incumbency and inherent difficulty for challengers to achieve change affects all newcomers, women prominently among them. Since incumbents overwhelmingly are men, there is not much of a chance for women to break in unless they are willing to be forceful challengers and some examples of success exist.

I am very grateful to Mr. Pranav Gupta, Director of MD Publications Pvt Ltd, New Delhi, for his kind cooperation and support for this book.

A K Yadav

CONTENTS

1

Politics

An Introduction

Politics is the process by which groups of people make decisions. The term is generally applied to behaviour within civil governments, but politics has been observed in all human group interactions, including corporate, academic, and religious institutions. It consists of "social relations involving authority or power" and refers to the regulation of a political unit, and to the methods and tactics used to formulate and apply policy.

"Politics" ultimately comes from the Greek word "polis" meaning state or city. "Politikos" describes anything concerning the state or city affairs. In Latin, this was "politicus" and in French "politique". Thus it became "politics" in the English language.

AS AN ACADEMIC DISCIPLINE

Political science, the study of politics, examines the acquisition and application of power. Related areas of study include political philosophy, which seeks a rationale for politics and an ethic of public behaviour, political economy, which attempts to develop understandings of the relationships between politics and the economy and the governance of the two, and public administration, which examines the practices of governance. Politic- to move and advance a particular move or need in detriment to the opposing view or need and also an attempt to gain or maintain control over a limited resource.

SPECTRA

Left-right Politics

Recently in history, political analysts and politicians divide politics into left wing and right wing politics, often also using the idea of center politics as a middle path of policy between the right and left. This classification is comparatively recent (it was not used by Aristotle or Hobbes, for instance), and dates from the French Revolution era, when those members of the National Assembly who opposed the monarchy sat on the left, while those who supported it sat on the right. The original meaning disappeared quickly. A particularly influential event was the publication of the Communist Manifesto by Karl Marx and Frederick Engels in 1848. The Manifesto suggested a course of action for a proletarian revolution to overthrow the bourgeois society and abolish private property, in the belief that this would lead to a classless and stateless society.

The meaning of left-wing and right-wing varies considerably between different countries and at different times, but generally speaking, it can be said that the right wing often values tradition and capitalism while the left wing often values egalitarianism.

According to Norberto Bobbio, one of the major exponents of this distinction, the Left believes in attempting to eradicate social inequality, while the Right regards most social inequality as the result of ineradicable natural inequalities, and sees attempts to enforce social equality as utopian or authoritarian.

Some ideologies, notably Christian Democracy, claim to combine left and right wing politics; according to Geoffrey K. Roberts and Patricia Hogwood, "In terms of ideology, Christian Democracy has incorporated many of the views held by liberals, conservatives and socialists within a wider framework of moral and Christian principles." Movements which claim or formerly claimed to be above the left-right divide include Gaullism in France, Peronism in Argentina, and National Action Politics in Mexico.

Authoritarian-libertarian Politics

For instance, classical liberalism (also known as *laissez-faire liberalism*, or, in much of the world, simply *liberalism*) is a doctrine stressing individual freedom and limited government. This includes the importance of human rationality, individual property rights, free markets, natural rights, the protection of civil liberties, constitutional limitation of government, and individual freedom from restraint as exemplified in the writings of John Locke, Adam Smith, David Hume, David Ricardo, Voltaire, Montesquieu and others. According to the libertarian Institute for Humane Studies, "the libertarian, or 'classical liberal,' perspective is that individual well-being, prosperity, and social harmony are fostered by 'as much liberty as possible' and 'as little government as necessary.'"

WOMEN IN POLITICS

Women have historically been underrepresented in Western socities compared to men. Many women, however, have been politically elected to be heads of state and government. Most prominent may be the female leaders of world powers such as Prime Minister of the United Kingdom Margaret Thatcher, Prime Minister of India Indira Gandhi, Prime Minister of Israel Golda Meir, Chancellor of Germany Angela Merkel, Prime Minister of Canada Kim Campbell, Prime Minister of France Edith Cresson, President of the People's Republic of China Soong Ching-ling (AKA Rosamond Soong), and Director of the Cultural Revolution, dictator Jiang Qing.

EXECUTIVE BRANCH OF GOVERNMENT

The first women other than monarchs to hold head of state positions were in socialist countries. The first was Khertek Anchimaa-Toka of the Tuvan People's Republic from 1940-1944, followed by Sükhbaataryn Yanjmaa of the Mongolian People's Republic 1953-1954 and Soong Ching-ling of the People's Republic of China from 1968-1972 and 1981.

Following the socialist countries, the Nordic countries have been forerunners in including women in the executive branch. The second cabinet Brundtland (1986-1989) was historical in that 8 out of 18 cabinet members were women, and in 2007 the second cabinet Stoltenberg (2005-present) was more than 50% women. Some current female politicians that have reached top positions in the Nordic countries are the President of Finland, Tarja Halonen and Deputy Prime Minister of Sweden, Maud Olofsson.

The world's first elected female president was Vigdís Finnbogadóttir of Iceland, whose term lasted from 1980 to 1996.

In 2005, Ellen Johnson-Sirleaf of Liberia became Africa's first elected female head of state.

LEGISLATIVE BRANCH OF GOVERNMENT

It was not until World War I and the first socialist revolutions that the first few women became members of governments. Alexandra Kollontai became the first female to hold a minister position, as the People's Commissar for Social Welfare in Soviet Russia in 1917. Nina Bang, Danish Minister of Education from 1924-26, was the world's second full female cabinet minister.

The first female head of government was Evgeniia Bosh, the Bolshevik military leader who held the People's Secretary of Internal Affairs position in the Ukraine People's Republic of the Soviets of Workers and Peasants from 1917-1918, which was responsible for executive functions. Nevertheless, development was slow and it was not until the end of the 20th century that female ministers stopped being unusual.

The first government organization formed with the goal of women's equality was the Zhenotdel, started by the government of Soviet Russia.

According to a 2006 report by the Inter-Parliamentary Union, 16% of all parliament members in the world are female. In 1995, the United Nations set a goal of 30%. The top ten countries are Rwanda with 56.3%, Sweden (47.0%), Cuba

(43.2%), Finland (41.5%), the Netherlands (41.3%), Argentina (40.0%), Denmark (38.0%), Angola (37.3%), Costa Rica (36.8%), and Spain (36.3%). Cuba has the highest percentage for countries without a quota.

According to the same report, nine countries have no women parliament members.

The US House of Representatives contains 77 women, and the US Senate contains 16. Eight states have female governors. See also: Women in the United States House of Representatives, Women in the United States Senate, and List of female state governors in the United States.

WOMEN IN POLITICS: GOOD NEWS AND BAD

Women in politics grabbed headlines this week with a new report from the National Council of State Legislators that showed their numbers mushrooming in state leadership. Surely the gain in the number of women leaders of state legislative chambers is to be duly noted and celebrated, as is the increasing movement of women into national political leadership but not without accompanying cautionary footnotes.

First the good news. In 2007, The Associated Press reports, 58 women were chosen to lead their state senates, houses and assemblies, a record number and a terrific sign of building momentum. It means female politicians will take charge of important segments of states' tax and spending decisions, have a greater say in state government's political priorities and even help the women behind them move into more powerful political state positions.

The AP tells us the number of female senate presidents, house speakers and presidents pro tem at 58 this year is a 20 percent gain over last year's tally of 48 and "more than double the (number of) female leaders in 2000. At just 17 percent of all state legislative leaders, that's about one out of six. It is far from reflecting the overall U.S. population; women make up slightly more than half of all Americans."

And therein lies the bad news. While amassing impressive

gains in leadership positions, women's actual representation in state legislatures is hung, as it has been, below 25 percent. Despite a slight gain in the overall percentage this year - to 23.5 percent - many legislatures see the numbers slipping. Last month the AP reported, "Women lost ground in 20 of 50 statehouses following the November election. This year, 17.4 percent of the Ohio Legislature is female, down from 18.4 percent in 2006."

Still, those numbers trounce women's representation in Congress, which stands at 16 percent in the Senate (16 among 100 senators total) and about the same percentage, or 71, in the 435-member House.

From a historical perspective, women's gains in statehouses are little short of astonishing. In the late 1970s, there were four women total. But the geometric rises of the 1980s and early '90s slowed to a crawl at the turn of the millennium. For the longest time, conservatives' claims that fewer women were running for office because more were choosing to become full-time homemakers.

But there was another huge factor at work: term limits. The original purpose of term limits was to open up the political process to people who had been frozen out. But Debbie Walsh, director of Rutgers University's Center for American Women and Politics told the AP: "There was a power in incumbency. Women would get in and 98 percent of the time they would get re-elected, so you just needed a few new women in each time.... But with term limits, you get this wholesale loss of women and you've got to get a whole lot to run to make up for it."

Let us hope those women state leaders, and their counterparts on the national scene - such as House Speaker Nancy Pelosi and Democratic presidential contender Hillary Rodham Clinton - use their newfound power wisely. It's common knowledge female lawmakers generally place more importance on health, education and public welfare issues. But let's hope this new generation of women leaders couples this new set of priorities with a strong sense of fiscal priorities to keep spending in check.

Women political leaders have a terrific opportunity to show the nation they can not only run government better, they can run it cheaper and spare the taxpayer. Pelosi, a California Democrat, has shown early indications of fiscal responsibility with her renewed emphasis on House members who propose legislation that increases spending must show where they will cut the budget elsewhere to pay for new costs. It's an example all women state leaders need to follow.

WOMAN IN POLITICS: THE GLASS CEILING

One of the many programs at the League's November 2003 conference in Atlantic City was titled "Why Aren't There More Women in New Jersey Politics?" Nothing has happened since then to change the appropriateness of asking that question again in 2004. But, it is a loaded question. The use of the word "more" implies that there are not enough women in politics and that there might be a right or adequate number. Each person could probably come up with a different assessment.

Since women make up more than 50 percent of the total population, one standard might be that women should hold half the elected positions, but obviously there is no agreement on what is the right number or the number that might indicate progress in achieving better representation.

Given its education and income level of the state's population, New Jerseyans might expect that women would comprise a larger percentage of elective officials in their state. Another aspect is what appears to be the "pipeline problem." The low number of women mayors raises questions about how well the base is built for women to move on to higher office. On the other hand, more than a third of the county offices are held by women, but apparently this does not lead to moving on to the legislature.

NEED WOMEN IN GOVERNMENT

In discussing numbers of women in office, the question arises about why we should care that more women serve in elected positions. Three ways of answering that question are: it is fair; society needs their talents; and, they make a difference.

The matter of fairness becomes particularly important when addressing the barriers to women achieving elective office and raises the questions of why they are not included in an affirmative manner. As for talent, this concept, which encompasses knowledge and experience, recognizes that women have a demonstrated track record of educational achievement, and leadership in political and civic affairs that is useful to society and therefore should not be ignored. Making a difference means that having women elected officials shapes a different outcome in the public policy process. Research studies, including seminal studies conducted by the Center for American Women and Politics, show that "despite differences in party control, political climate, and ideology...., the presence of women made a difference in shaping the terms of debate and in the public policy outcomes...."

WHAT WOMEN DO TO INCREASE THE NUMBERS?

The concept of "more" also implies that there are actions that can be taken to up the percentages of women holding elective office. Once women achieved the right to vote, the next effort was to promote the women's role in government and prepare them for public office.

The strategies to do so take three main courses: focus on younger girls in high school and college to introduce them to women who are role models and encourage their involvement in politics; provide opportunities for women to get information, training and support for running for office; and, promote the appointment of women in politics and government to give them experience and visibility for pursuing elective office as well as political leadership. In New Jersey, many different groups have taken up the cause. For example, Republican women organized the Christy Todd Whitman Excellence in Public Service Series to train about 20 women each year to become active politically. Eagleton's Center for American Women and Politics has programs that focus on all three ways of improving women's participation in political life.

The new leadership program educates and empowers college women to participate actively in politics and public policy making through a well structured week-long session. Begun in New Jersey, the concept has spread to a number of other colleges around the country.

Ready to Run is a day-long program to help New Jersey women get the political skills they need to run for office. The next session is scheduled for Saturday, April 24.

And, since its inception in 1980, the Bi-Partisan Coalition for Women Appointments, staffed by CAWP, has encouraged women to submit their names for appointment to State government positions, boards and commissions and brought names to the attention of the Governor. It has also advocated for the appointment of women and assessed the record of appointing women.

What are the Barriers?

Given all the efforts women have organized to attain political office and the evidence they have marshaled that women's involvement makes a difference, why doesn't it happen? The reasons are probably imbedded in our political structure. The strength of incumbency and inherent difficulty for challengers to achieve change affects all newcomers, women prominently among them. Since incumbents overwhelmingly are men, there is not much of a chance for women to break in unless they are willing to be forceful challengers and some examples of success exist.

In addition, New Jersey still has both a strong tradition and laws that leave the decisions of who runs to the chairs of the county political parties, nearly all held by men. Women report that without women in leadership roles, the old boys' network will continue to favor those with whom they are familiar and in many cases have groomed. The nature of campaigns themselves nasty and negative may discourage women's participation. They wonder why anyone would want to be part of the current mode of political campaigning. Consequently, women are seeking other routes for public involvement through non-profit organizations and issue-oriented campaigns.

Finally, raising money has often been cited as a reason women don't enter into politics or don't succeed at it, but recent studies by national organizations, Emily's List (Democrats) and Wish List (Republicans), show that if women are given the chance to run, they get financial support and they generate it successfully.

The More Question Gets Different Answers

For the moderator of the November League program, Phyllis Marchand, the Mayor of Princeton Township and the panelists, State Senator Shirley Turner, Kim Ricketts, former member of the Highland Park Council and former Assemblywoman Ginny Weber, the answer was clear. Yes, women elected officials are critically important participants in New Jersey's political life and there should be more. The same response came from the large and enthusiastic crowd that made up the audience. The response from outside the room at Convention Hall, while not heard and documented, is probably not as firm or committed to change and clearly plays a big role in answering the "more" question.

UNMARRIED WOMEN ARE A SURGING FORCE IN AMERICAN POLITICS

USA - Every year this nation's priorities move further and further away from the concerns of the majority of American citizens, making daily life harder and harder. The prices we pay for housing, utilities, medications, transportation and food are all going up. Meanwhile, big business interests, profiting every time we lose, monopolize our policymakers' attention. While companies boasting record profits are rewarded with tax breaks, ordinary citizens struggle each day to get basic needs met for themselves and their families.

Wouldn't it be wonderful if all Americans hurt by Washington's lopsided economic policies banded together to form a voting bloc; and, like the religious right of elections past, became a force with the power to determine this election and all elections from this year on? Well, according to Page Gardener, one of the nation's top strategists and an expert in the voting patterns of women, a unique voting bloc such as this *does* exist. Despite their poor voter turnout in years past, Gardener says that unmarried women in this country are fed up. They are united, and they are ready to vote.

The striking economic circumstance of unmarried women when compared to their married counterparts begins with income. While 44% of unmarried women live in households of incomes of $30,000 or less, 44% of married women live in households earning $75,000 or more. The majority of households in this country are now headed by an unmarried person - single Americans caring for children, elderly parents, and other dependants.

They are economically stretched - one out of five unmarried women in this country has no healthcare and half of all children six and under who live with unmarried mothers are living in poverty. As Page Gardener put it, "This is an indictment." Policy makers are reckless to ignore this economic reality. When this group mobilizes they will discover that they have to address unmarried women's concerns if they want to stay in office.

According to Gardener, unmarried women are "sick of the way things are going, and they want this country to go in a new direction." These women feel America is not doing enough about problems on the home front, the problems most significant in their lives. They struggle financially, their lives are difficult, and they want our leaders to make them a national priority. The good news, Gardener finds, is that they are making their voices heard in record numbers at the voting booth. In 2006 they were the largest "change" voters. As their power becomes more evident, it will be harder and harder for policy makers to ignore their calls for adequate housing, healthcare, and other domestic issues affecting them.

While domestic issues are the primary concern of unmarried women voters, like married women, they are incredibly patriotic and concerned about this country. They are concerned about family values, security issues and they mirror the concerns of the total population in many ways. As this population grows, however, it is their unique economic circumstances that set them apart and which creates the huge and growing cohort. "We've got this enormous growing demographic group and they have an agenda on their own, they are redefining the electorate, and they are redefining how we should look at America and the public policy agenda of our elected officials," Gardener told me.

The *Women Vote* has found that 91% of the unmarried women voters they surveyed reported that their frustration with public policy made them more likely to vote in 2008. They are paying attention and are interested in record numbers. Polling data reported on their website shows that 64% of unmarried women voters usually considered unlikely to vote (eligible and registered, but who missed at least one of the last two presidential elections) now say they are "absolutely certain" to vote in 2008. Women's Voices. Women Vote also found 77% of unmarried women voters are expressing a high level of interest in this election. "Unmarrieds, even those who don't normally vote, are primed for this election and are open to politicians willing to engage them on issues important to them."

Last week's caucus in Iowa, according to a January 4 press release, serves as an indication that unmarried women are in fact utilizing their power. Unmarried Women Caucus in Record Numbers reported that unmarried women did turn out in numbers greater than their overall share of Iowa's population – a feat only married women used to achieve. "While unmarried women are 22 percent of the eligible voting age population in Iowa, network entrance polls report that they were 28 percent of participants in the Democratic caucus...Married women, by contrast, were in line with their proportion of the overall population, accounting for 29 percent of the eligible population in Iowa, and accounting for 29% of Democratic caucus attendees." (Statistics from the Republican contest had not yet been released at the time of this press release.) According to Gardener, "The 28% of Iowan women on their own who caucused is the first example of the critical role unmarried women will play in the national discussion, demanding the attention of the Presidential candidates."

Women's Voices. Women Vote has made the significant discovery that unmarried women are "a surging force in American politics." Their power is not only in their numbers but also in their unified desire for change. In my conversation with Page Gardner, it came as no surprise to learn that her organization will have successfully registered over a million unmarried women during this election cycle. We can all do our part by joining Women's Voices. Women Vote's online campaign "20 million Reasons" and help register unmarried women to vote. Page Gardener also pointed out that it is important for media organizations like The WIP to write about unmarried women in America. "As these women see their lives reflected in the conversation around civic participation through articles in the newspaper, through the media...it is validating and is also motivating. So, the more that we can reflect their lives and say... 'we know you are out there, we know how powerful you are,' the better, in terms of getting them to participate." If unmarried women voted at the same rate as married women, over six million more voters would have gone to the polls in 2004.

POLITICS SUITABLE FOR WOMEN

Being in power is not a pleasurable or entertaining game. But the fame and money draws both men and women into politics. Lot of questions has arisen about women becoming politicians. Men think that women are gentle and kind and this profession will not suit their character. But men's attitudes have changed now that women have proved in their jobs and have climbed up the political ladder. To rise to the top of the field dominated by men is not so easy. It is said that in Rwanda, where, 14 years after a massacre left nearly one million people dead, women make up nearly half of parliament;

In India, the All India Anna Dravida Munnetra Kazhagam (AIADMK) set an example by making a conscious move to bring many more women into decision-making levels and posts within the party.

It is said that very little has changed for Indian women in Politics since Independence and women are still a political minority. What may be the causes?

Some ridicule women saying they may not have time for politics because they need more time to make up rather than concentrating on serious issues. How unfair to women!

Also, women helping other women are a rarity and so they would not allow other women to enter into their parties.

Joke apart, politics was a respectable profession but now it has turned into opportunism and invariably politicians are looked at, with contempt. This may be a reason for women to hesitate to come forward to enter into politics.

Days which are spent away from the family is possibly more than that in any other profession. The crippling impact is mind boggling.

They are forced to meet the complex demands of household management as well, just like any other profession. Women are more sentimental and emotional then men. Menaka Gandhi is an example of one such woman. She could not help but talk about motherhood when her son Varun Gandhi was arrested.

There is no privacy for women politicians because politics is being portrayed as an entertaining game by the media and washing linen in public is a very common aspect of politics. Misreporting by the media may sometime create havoc in the family relationship. Women have to face this issue if they become politicians because they are compelled to project themselves in the media for gaining votes.

Terrorists aim for the lives of politicians and women cannot afford to risk their lives because they are tied up to their families as well. Smt. Indira Gandhi will naturally occupy our minds when we talk about gunmen and politicians.

Despite these setbacks and risks, women are climbing up the political ladder. Things have started looking good for women, in the political arena. Many women, educated and elite are entering into politics with interest, though they seem to be a minority as of now. It is a brave, new world for them.

Sonia Gandhi is a dynamic leader now even though it was the influence of the dynastic charisma at first. Though Mayavathi and Jayalalitha depended on other political leaders for rising up, now they are significant leaders in their own rights, even though both of them are said to possess assets disproporationate to their income. Mamta Banerjee was another gutsy politician who took advantage of political opportunism. Sheila Dixit, Bharathi and Raje are yet another few women politicians who are prominent.

In international politics, we have heard of Hillary Clinton, Benazir Bhutto and the likes while Indian women like Mayawathi and Jayalalitha, make themselves heard in the political forefront in India. But how long can these elite, high class women pull forward the ordinary lower and middle class of women? One can only wait and see how many more women of substance will enter politics and make the gender proud!

MEN OR WOMEN: WHO'S THE BETTER LEADER

Americans believe women have the right stuff to be political leaders. When it comes to honesty, intelligence and a handful of other character traits they value highly in leaders, the public rates women superior to men, according to a new nationwide Pew Research Center Social and Demographic Trends survey.

Nevertheless, a mere 6% of respondents in this survey of 2,250 adults say that, overall, women make better political leaders than men. About one-in-five (21%) say men make the better leaders, while the vast majority - 69% - says men and women make equally good leaders.

The paradox embedded in these survey findings is part of a wider paradox in modern society on the subject of gender and leadership.

In an era when women have made sweeping strides in educational attainment and workforce participation, relatively few have made the journey all the way to the highest levels of political or corporate leadership.

Why not? In the survey, the public cites gender discrimination, resistance to change, and a self-serving "old boys club" as reasons for the relative scarcity of women at the top. In somewhat smaller numbers, respondents also say that women's family responsibilities and their shortage of experience hold them back from the upper ranks of politics and business.

What the public does not say is that women inherently lack what it takes to be leaders. To the contrary, on seven of eight leadership traits measured in this survey, the public rates women either better than or equal to men.

For example, half of all adults say women are more honest than men, while just one-in-five say men are more honest (the rest say they don't know or volunteer the opinion that there's no difference between the sexes on this trait). And honesty, according to respondents, is the most important to leadership of any of the traits measured in the survey.

The next most important leadership trait, in the public's view, is intelligence. Here again, women outperform men: 38% of respondents say women are smarter than men, while just 14% say men are smarter, and the remainder say there's no difference between the sexes.

Men and women tie on two of the next three traits on the public's ranking of leadership qualities measured in this survey - hard work and ambition. Men prevail over women on decisiveness (their lone "victory" in the battery of eight traits), with 44% of respondents saying that men are more decisive and 33% saying women are.

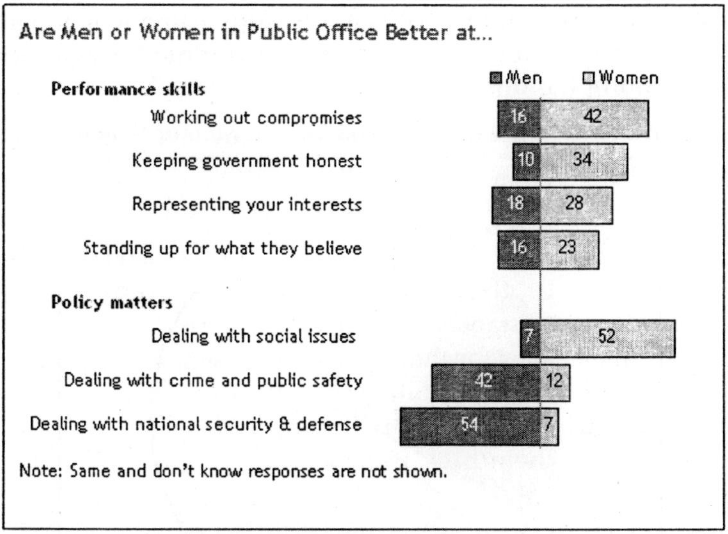

Finally, women have big leads over men on the last three traits on the public's rankings of the eight items measured: being compassionate (80% say women; 5% say men); being outgoing (47% say women; 28% say men) and being creative (62% say women; 11% say men).

For anyone keeping score, that's women over men by five to one, with two ties, on eight traits, each of which at least two-thirds of the public says is very important or absolutely essential to leadership. Notably, nearly all of these gender evaluations are shared by men as well as women, though the margins are more heavily pro-woman among female respondents than among male respondents.

The survey also asked respondents to assess whether men or women in public office are better at handling a range of policy matters and job performance challenges. On the policy front, women are widely judged to be better than men at dealing with social issues such as health care and education, while men have a big edge over women in the public's perception of the way they deal with crime, public safety, defense and national security.

As for job performance skills, women get higher marks than men in all of the measures tested: standing up for one's principles in the face of political pressure; being able to work out compromises; keeping government honest; and representing the interests of "people like you."

Who makes a Better Political Leader: Men or Women?

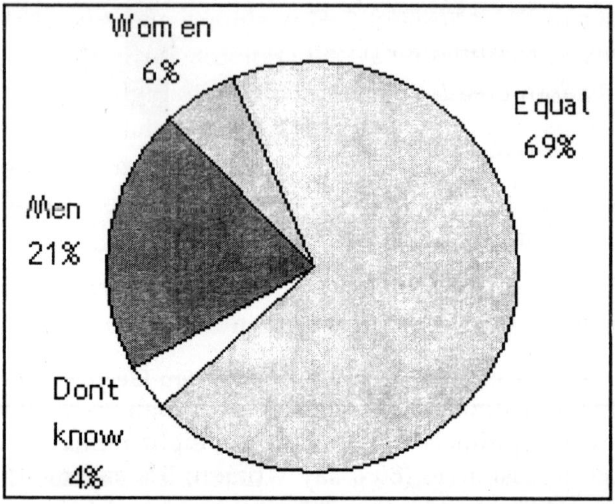

Overall, however, women emerge from this survey a bit like a sports team that racks up better statistics but still loses the game - witness the tiny 6% sliver of the public that says women generally make better political leaders than men.

To be sure, the fact that such a large majority of respondents (69%) say that women and men make equally good political leaders is itself a measure of the profound changes in women's role in society that have taken place over the past several decades.

Women make up 57% of all college students, about half of all law and medical school students, and more than four-in-ten students who earn masters degrees in business. They make up 46% of the total private sector workforce and 38% of all managers. However, it's still lonely for women at the very highest rungs of the corporate and political ladder. Women are just 2% of the CEOs of the nation's Fortune 500 companies. In the political realm, they make up just 17% of all members of the U.S. House of Representatives; 16% of all U.S. senators; 16% of all governors; and 24% of all state legislators.

Internationally, the U.S.ranks in the middle range - 85th in the world - in its share of women in the lower house of its national legislative body.

Asked what accounts for this slow movement toward gender parity in top political positions, about half (51%) of all survey respondents say a major reason is that Americans simply aren't ready to elect a woman to high office; more than four-in-ten (43%) say a major reason is that women who are active in politics are held back by men, and 38% say a major reason is that women are discriminated against in all realms of society, and politics is no exception.

These are the three most prevalent choices among seven possible explanations presented in the survey.

Why Aren't there more Women in top Elective Office?

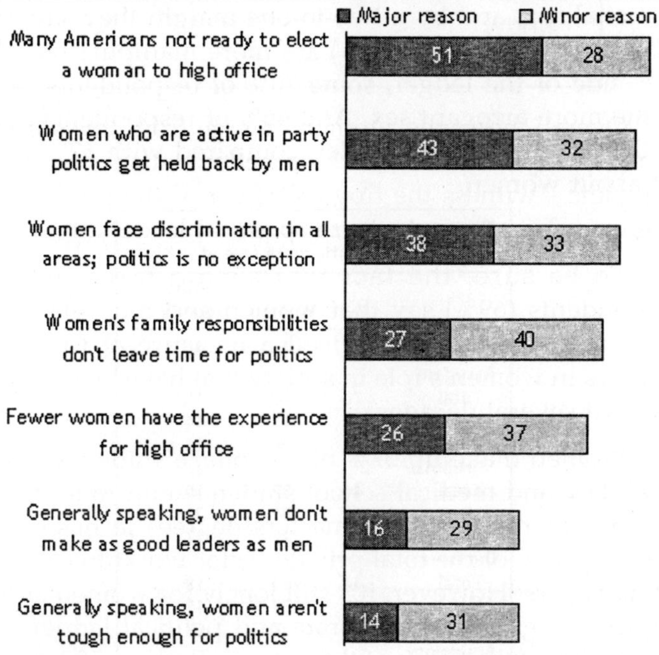

Note: Not a reason and don't know responses are not shown.

Next in the pecking order of explanations is the time pressure that comes with trying to balance work and family; 27% of the public cites this as a major reason there aren't more women leaders in politics.

Some 26% say that a big reason is that women don't have the experience required for higher office. The least common explanations - chosen as a major reason by just 16% and 14% of respondents, respectively - are that women don't make as good leaders as men and those women aren't tough enough for politics.

OTHER KEY FINDINGS FROM THE SURVEY

Negative Gender Stereotypes: In addition to asking about the eight leadership traits, the survey asked about four traits that are often viewed in a negative light. By a lopsided margin, respondents say that women (85%), not men (5%), are the more emotional sex, and by a two-to-one margin they say women (52%) rather than men (26%) are more manipulative. On the other side of the ledger, some 70% of respondents say men are the more arrogant sex. And 46% of respondents say men are the more stubborn gender, compared with 32% who say that about women.

Traits of Men and Women
Is this characteristic more true of...

	Men	Women	Both, equally
	%	%	%
Arrogant			
Total	70	10	15
Men	69	11	14
Women	71	9	16
Stubborn			
Total	46	32	19
Men	40	34	21
Women	52	29	17
Decisive			
Total	44	33	18
Men	48	29	19
Women	40	37	17
Ambitious			
Total	34	34	29
Men	40	27	30
Women	29	39	28

Outgoing			
Total	28	47	22
Men	32	41	23
Women	24	52	21
Hardworking			
Total	28	28	41
Men	34	21	41
Women	23	35	40
Manipulative			
Total	26	52	16
Men	21	57	16
Women	32	48	16
Honest			
Total	20	50	24
Men	23	45	27
Women	17	56	21
Intelligent			
Total	14	38	43
Men	18	33	43
Women	10	43	43
Creative			
Total	11	62	24
Men	14	54	28
Women	8	68	20
Compassionate			
Total	5	80	13
Men	7	78	14
Women	3	83	12
Emotional			
Total	5	85	9
Men	7	83	9
Women	3	87	9

Note: Don't know responses not shown.

Gender Solidarity

In this survey, women see themselves in a more favorable light than men see women. Likewise, men see themselves in a better light than women see men. However, for men, gender solidarity goes only so far.

Overall, they give their gender the better ratings on just five of the 12 traits (decisiveness; hard work; ambition; not being emotional; not being manipulative) and they give themselves inferior ratings on seven (honesty; intelligence; compassion; creativity; being outgoing; being stubborn; being arrogant). By contrast, while women say they are more emotional and more manipulative than men, they give themselves higher marks than men on the 10 other traits measured.

Gender and Race

Of all demographic groups, black women are distinctive in the degree to which they say women are superior to men in their evaluations of character traits.

Nearly eight-in-ten (78%) black women (compared with 51% of white women and 50% of all adults) say women are more honest than men. About two-thirds (65%) of black women (compared with 37% of white women and 38% of all adults) say women are smarter than men. And about half (49%) of black women (compared with 33% of white women and 28% of all adults) say women are more hardworking than men.

Twice as Hard; Half as Far

The feminist rallying cry that women have to work twice as hard to get half as far as men in their careers find some statistical support from this survey as least with regard to leadership evaluations. Survey respondents who rate men better than women on key character traits have a sharply increased likelihood of saying that men make better political leaders than women. But respondents who rate women better than men on these same traits have only a slightly increased likelihood of saying women make better leaders than men.

It's a Man's World

By a ratio of nearly two-to-one, Americans say that, all things considered, men rather than women have a better life in this country.

Women believe this in greater numbers than men do, and younger and middle-aged adults believe it in greater numbers than older adults do. The view that men have the better life than women is not as strong now as it was 15 years ago, when the public said by a ratio of about three-to-one that men had the better life. However, still farther back in time, attitudes were much different. In 1972, during the early days of the modern gender revolution, slightly more adults said women had the better life than said that about men.

Generational Differences among Women

Older women are more inclined than younger women to see the need for more social change to ensure that women have equal rights; seven-in-ten women ages 50 and over say more change is needed, a view shared by just 53% of women ages 18-29. At the same time, younger and middle-aged women are more inclined than older women to say that men rather than women have the better life in this country.

Discrimination and Equal Rights

A majority of adults (57%) say the nation needs to continue to make changes to give women equal rights with men. A similar majority (54%) says discrimination against women is either a serious or somewhat serious problem in society. However, a bigger majority (63%) says that discrimination against blacks is a serious or somewhat serious problem.

Admiration for Hillary Clinton

The survey asked no questions about Sen. Hillary Clinton or the 2008 presidential campaign. However, in answer to an open-ended question, Clinton and Sen.Barack Obama were each named by 13% of respondents as the political figure in the U.S. that they admire most. President Bush was the third most frequently mentioned figure, named by 7% of respondents. Women are more than twice as likely as men to name Clinton as the figure they admire most; and Hispanics are much more likely than blacks and somewhat more likely than whites to name her as the figure they admire most.

DO WOMEN MAKE BETTER LEADERS THAN MEN

Is leadership gender neutral, or does gender matter? Are men better at the leadership thing in practice, or do women having better leadership attributes in theory?

An outsider, studying our culture from the headlines on business and news magazines, might wonder what all the fuss is about. Women wanted the top jobs, then they got them, then they didn't want them anymore. Men wanted to keep women out, then they thought that becoming more feminine would give them a competitive advantage, then they got tough and ruthless all over again. Now women are nearly as ubiquitous as men in the middle management ranks, and there are enough women making an impact at the "C" level that no one can label them token representatives anymore. But while things may look slightly better in terms of numbers, something is still not quite right below the surface. Male or female, gender isn't supposed to matter in the corporate setting anymore. So how come the bulk of the research out there points to the same ugly problems concerning women in leadership?

You see, ever since the industrial revolution - or at least the 1930s - the organization had been markedly masculine. The dominant "mechanical school" of organizational theory, for example, was founded on such ideas as centralized authority, specialization and expertise, division of labor, principles, rules, and regulations. The emerging organization, however, was more feminine in gender because it was characterized by collaboration, the delegation of authority, empowerment, trust, openness, concern for the whole person, an emphasis on interpersonal relations, and the inevitability of interdependence. The type of organization that would appear to be the perfect platform for what Dr. Lois Frankel calls the "feminization of leadership". In her instructive book, See Jane Lead (2007), Frankel states that women have always lead, but not in ways that were valued or recognized in the old, mechanical school. Women, it would seem, were finally in the right place at the right time

SO SOFT IT'S HARD

With a flattened organizational structure, and a knowledge economy that put a premium on such feminine characteristics as collaboration, trust and sensitivity, it was only a matter of time before some social psychologist decided to start grooming men in a new way. After all these years, men were now told that hard skills were not really that important when it came to leadership. Technical attributes were like tool belts; they could be picked up at the hardware store when needed, and strapped on to suit the task at hand. Being smart was way less important than being emotionally intelligent.

According to writers like Daniel Goleman, women have emotional intelligence in spades. All that time spent chatting instead of getting to the crux of important issues? That was really about bonding, openness, sharing, empathy, building rapport, and trust. How about the need to consult everyone in the organization from the boss to the janitor before making an important decision? That was all about consensus building, alignment, and seeing the issue from multiple perspectives.

During the boom years, it seemed to work. Productivity was high, stock prices rose, new markets emerged and old markets got bigger and more profitable. Maybe this business of the organization and leadership becoming feminine wasn't so bad after all? Then the bubble burst, the economy contracted, and long-range projections for growth fell off a cliff. Time to baton down the hatches. After all, when the going gets tough the tough get going.

That's when women started to reconsider what I call "ROL", or Return on Leadership.

WHO'S SORRY NOW?

When the going got tough, a lot of women decided they didn't want to be any tougher. All of that slaving for the big bucks, working yourself to the bone, ripping the fabric of your family and personal life to shreds... maybe it just wasn't worth it; the ROL was in the "red" for many talented women. The headlines on those business and news magazines said it all. Women Aren't In The Corner Office, They Don't Want Power, They're Opting Out... magazines like Fortune, FastCompany, and the New York Times Magazine exclaimed. Warren Farrell's taboo-busting book, Why Men Earn More, laid it out straight: women tend to put in less time than men, working fewer hours; and, statistically, people who work 44 hours a week make almost twice as much as those who work 34 hours. As a result, women still comprise fewer than 2% of Fortune 1000 CEO's and just 7.9% of Fortune 500 top earners.

As an article in the Wall Street Journal (10/24/05) pointed out, the reasons are many; "women hit their prime child bearing years at the same time they are most pressured to prove themselves at work; they are reluctant to put in the 80-hour work week and globe trotting required for the corner office; they are too concentrated on staff positions like HR and marketing, where they never learn P&L responsibility; and they don't have informed mentoring and networking opportunities, like golfing with the guys.

These theories belie a consistent finding in the research - there is little difference between the leadership abilities of successful male and female bosses. Carol Hymowitz of the WSJ hit it right on the head when she states, "the big problem is both sexes believe their own biased perceptions more than they believe [the facts]." To be sure, I, and a number of researchers, realize that women still face an inherent bias in or society, adding to the challenges that Alice Eagly and Linda Carli describe in their HBR article (September 2007) Women and The Labyrinth of Leadership. In the language of psychologists, they state that the clash is between two sets of associations: "communal and agentic". Women are still associated with communal traits, which denote compassion and affection, whereas men are associated with agentic, or dominant, self reliant, and confident traits; core to the traditional notion of leadership.

For all of these reasons and theories, research organizations like Catalyst claimed that women were leaving Fortune 500 companies at an astounding 1400 women per day rate. Where they were going was anyone's guess, but given the level of heated discussion over the issue of work-life balance, we can imagine that they were sick of the grind. Maybe power wasn't worth it? Maybe the glass ceiling was more like plexiglass protection around a violent hockey game? Or maybe the women are not getting the intellectual stimulation they need, or, as a May 1, 2005 article in the New York Times decided, they are just bored. ("Behind the Exodus of Executive Women: Boredom.")

Frankly, many men are beginning to analyze their ROL

as well, and coming to the same conclusions that apparently many women have come too. In a study conducted by Burson and Marsteller, in 2001, 27% of Senior Executives said they are not interested in becoming CEO. In 2005, over 60% said they are not interested. I would only assume that this percentage has risen significantly again in the last two years.

ON THE FOLLY OF HOPING FOR "A" WHILE REWARDING "B"

The true nature of our problem, in my opinion, is explained best in Steve Kerr's famous essay, "On the Folly of Hoping for 'A' While Rewarding 'B'." Kerr described a common problem in HR development initiatives. We say we want "X" but we persist in rewarding "Y." Consider the case of the feminization of leadership. A whole generation of leaders - men and women alike - were developed on the notion that sensitive, caring, coalition-building characteristics would lead to success. Open your arms, give your employees a big hug, explain everything they ever wanted to know about your motivations and underlying objectives, empower them, set them free, and they will perform for you at unprecedented levels, thereby securing your ultimate goals. It's a win-win-win situation.

Does it work like that in the real world? Well, as Ernest Hemingway once wrote, "Isn't it pretty to think so?"

In the real world, leadership is not always most effective when it is most caring, open, transparent, sensitive and empowering. In fact, fear, manipulation, ruthlessness, power-hoarding and the competitive will to win at all costs are common characteristics of our best, and most effective leaders. While that may not sound very warm and fuzzy, it cannot be ignored. The organization may have become more feminine in structure and culture at the dawn of the knowledge era; but business results remain unabashedly male. Leadership may have softened in the last decade, but getting to the top, and staying there once you've made it, remains a tough, hard, ruthless, and overtly political act.

If women are only talking to other women about the

struggles of leadership, and men are only talking to other men about "women" leaders, progress will continue to be slow. In Eagly and Carli's HBR article referenced earlier, they state that women have traditionally "underinvested" in social capital. They cite a study that suggests that social capital is even more necessary to a manager's advancement than "the skillful performance of traditional managerial tasks." The emphasis that the "social networks" need to comprise both men and women if greater understanding (and thus, appreciation) among the sexes is to be achieved. Women have traditionally complained that 'breaking" into the "good ole' boy's" network meant that they learn to play golf, drink Scotch, and have an occasional lunch at Hooters. Let me just state plainly; if these are the mores of the leadership within the company you want to advance in, you probably do need to learn "to play the game." Let me also state that this applies as much to men as to women. I have coached several male executives over the years who were faced with the same challenge, and who opposed going to Hooter's, hated golf, and preferred Chardonnay over Scotch... and my counsel was the same for them... learn the game or find an organization that more closely reflects your values, hobbies, and preferences.

Make it known that it's your intent to become a leader in your organization. So many men and women alike engage in what I call "hinting and hoping" around their aspiration to become a leader. When a female partner let us know that she wanted to become a leader in our firm, and that she also intended on having a family, we were all able to help her manage her "path to partner" much more effectively than if we all would have waited around and second guessed one another about the "what if's?" There were no surprises; we, the leaders in the firm, did not sit around and wonder if she was planning on leaving once she became pregnant, and we committed to providing feedback, coaching and mentoring, all focused around what she needed to do to become partner. Remember, if you have the skill and will to lead, and you make it known, you may find much greater support, which may even accelerate your path to leadership.

HOW THE WORLD RATES WOMEN AS LEADERS?

On December 10, Cristina Fernandez de Kirchner will be inaugurated as Argentina's first female president. The senator and first lady will join 11 other women who currently serve as their countries' presidents or prime ministers, including Michelle Bachelet in neighboring Chile. But while women worldwide are making gains in all levels of government, the most recent Pew Global Attitudes survey of 46 countries and the Palestinian territories finds that publics around the world express mixed opinions about women and political leadership.

The countries of Western Europe, North America and Latin America generally include the highest proportions of respondents who rate men and women as equally good political leaders. Roughly two-thirds in Kirchner's country (68%) express that view, while 17% say men are better leaders and 9% prefer women. In the United States, fully three-quarters say men and women make equally good political leaders, and that opinion is even more widespread in Western Europe.

By contrast, majorities in Mali (65%), the Palestinian territories (64%), Kuwait (62%), Pakistan (54%), Bangladesh (52%) and Ethiopia (51%) say men make better political leaders than women, as do nearly half of Jordanians (49%) and Nigerians (48%). Russians are also divided: 44% say men and women make equally good leaders while 40% say men are better. Only in Brazil do more people say women make better political leaders than say men do: 15% of Brazilians say women make better political leaders and 10% say men are better leaders.

Opinions about women in political leadership positions are somewhat correlated with the extent to which women play leadership roles, as measured by the World Economic Forum's political empowerment index. The index is derived from three sets of data: the ratio of women to men currently in cabinet-level positions in the country; the ratio of women to men in parliamentary positions, and the ratio of the number of years out of the last 50 in which the head of state was a woman to the number of years in which it was a man.

Publics in countries that receive the highest scores on the political empowerment scale are generally more likely to say that men and women make equally good political leaders. For example, in Sweden, the highest ranking country in terms of female political empowerment, fully nine-in-ten say men and women are equally good leaders. In Kuwait, on the other hand, where women were given the right to vote and to run for office for the first time in 2005, only one-third say men and women are equally good as political leaders while more than six-in-ten (62%) say men are better.

Political Empowerment and Views of Women in Political Leadership Positions

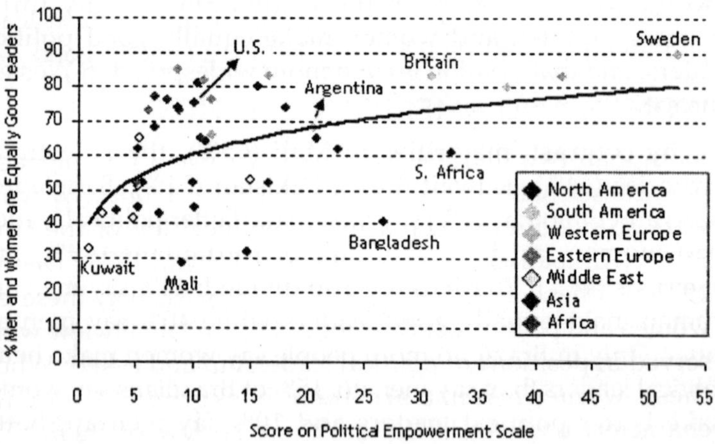

Plots represent 43 countries included in the 2007 Pew Global Attitudes Project and in the World Economic Forum's political empowerment index.
Correlation = .42

Views of political leadership often split along gender lines as well, with men more likely than women to say men make better political leaders and women more likely than men to say either that women make better leaders or that both are equally good. This is especially the case in Africa as well as in several Asian, Middle Eastern, and Eastern European countries. In Senegal, for example, a slight majority of men (51%) say men make better political leaders than women, but fewer than a quarter (23%) of Senegalese women share that view. Women in that country are much more likely to say both men and women are equally good as leaders (59% of women express that opinion vs. 37% of men).

In the United States, where Hillary Clinton currently leads the Democratic primary field in national polls, opinions about gender and political leadership reflect partisan rather than gender differences. Nearly three-in-ten (29%) Republicans say men make better leaders, compared with one-in-ten Democrats. A similar proportion of Democrats also say women would make better leaders (9%), and nearly eight-in-ten (78%) say both men and women are equally good. By contrast, only 2% of Republicans say women make better political leaders and about two-thirds (65%) say both are equally good.

WOMEN AND AMERICAN POLITICS

More than two decades have passed since a few pioneering political scientists began to raise questions about why women were so underrepresented in the political life of the United States (Kirkpatrick 1974; Tolchin and Tolchin 1976 ; Diamond 1977 ; Githens and Prestage 1977). In particular, these early women and politics scholars noticed that relatively few women served in positions of political leadership and asked: Who are these women? What are their backgrounds and their characteristics? And why are there so few of them? Their questions and their studies gave rise to more questions and more research, and over the years women and politics developed into a major area of scholarly inquiry within, and to a lesser extent outside, the discipline of political science.

We have learned a great deal during the past two decades about the participation of women in American politics, especially electoral politics which has been the focus of most research. As a result of studies conducted both by the Center for American Women and Politics (CAWP) 2 and by individual researchers, we now have considerable knowledge about the backgrounds of women who serve in public office in the United States, the obstacles they face in winning election, and their interests, attitudes, and priorities as officeholders (e.g., Johnson and Carroll 1978 ; Carroll and Strimling 1983 ; Dodson and Carroll 1991 ; Darcy, Welch, and Clark 1994 ; Carroll 1994 ; Burrell 1994 ; Gertzog 1995 ; Rosenthal 1998 ; Swers 2001; Carroll 2001). Similarly, research has greatly enhanced our understanding of the factors that facilitate and impede women's participation in other aspects of electoral politics-e.g., as voters and party activists (Freeman 2000 ; Sapiro 1983 ; Klein 1984 ; Burns, Schlozman, and Verba 2001 ; Schlozman, Burns, and Verba 1994).

However, while much has been learned over the past 25 years about women's participation in American politics, especially electoral politics, many questions remain. Developments in politics have presented new questions for scholars of women and politics. The number of women has increased substantially at some levels of office since the mid-1970s although women still remain vastly underrepresented at the highest levels. The increased numbers of women public officials have raised new questions about their potential impact: What difference, if any, does their presence make? To what extent have the increased numbers of women officeholders influenced public policy outcomes? Have women public officials helped to bring about noticeable changes in the political process or the way the business of politics is conducted? Under what circumstances do we see women in office making a difference? What effects do different institutional contexts and varying proportions of women among officeholders have on the extent to which women public officials has a distinctive, gender-related impact?

Similarly, the emergence (or at least public recognition) of gender differences in voting preferences, party identification, and other political attitudes and predispositions in the 1980s has posed a host of new questions for researchers.

To what extent do the gender differences evident since the 1980s represent new developments and to what extent are they simply old differences that previously had been overlooked? What political and social developments caused these differences? How can gender differences in voting behavior and political orientations be explained? And what is their political significance?

Major shifts in the political climate and changes in the political context also have raised new questions for women and politics researchers. For example, the euphoria among feminists following the election of record numbers of women to Congress in the 1992 elections, all of whom were pro-choice, quickly vanished in 1994 with the election of several right-wing, pro-life congresswomen. What motivates strongly conservative women to run for office? How do conservative women see their gender influencing their political priorities and behavior? What impact has the presence of more conservative women had on the ability of women public officials to advance a collective agenda? What are the implications of the increasing presence of right-wing women for theories of representation and how we conceptualize the relationship between the numbers of women in office and the representation of "women's interests?"

Talk radio and televised talk shows have played an increasingly important role in influencing political attitudes and perceptions in recent years, thereby raising new questions for women and politics scholars. Similarly, the Internet is fast becoming a key tool for communicating political messages, raising money in campaigns, and garnering information; yet, we know little about the ways this rapidly changing technology has influenced the political participation of women as voters and candidates. What effect have these media had on public attitudes toward politically active women? In what ways have they made the political climate more or less hospitable to women's involvement? Do gendered expectations about technology have an impact on its use by women candidates?

Just as political developments have raised new questions, so too have recent intellectual developments within the academy posed important challenges to women and politics researchers. The most important of these challenges have come from interdisciplinary feminist scholarship in the field of women's studies.

Most research on women and American politics has employed frameworks from political science and utilized scientific methodology, frequently relying on survey research. Because most of the existing work on women and politics has been conducted by scholars whose home discipline has viewed their research interests as marginal, the disciplinary and scientific orientation of much of the existing work on women and politics is understandable. In an attempt to achieve greater legitimacy for the study of women and politics and gain a foothold within their discipline, political scientists who study women and politics have generally adopted frameworks and methods favored by other political scientists. Yet, in striving for acceptance within political science, women and politics scholars have narrowed the range of questions they address, the frameworks they utilize, and the methods they employ.

Interdisciplinary feminist scholarship provides alternative frameworks to those that are prevalent in political science and can suggest different ways of thinking about the possible effects of gender on political behavior. For example, work by feminist historians on women's activism suggests that women have been politically active in ways and locations overlooked by political scientists and that political science operates with too narrow a definition of politics, centering on the electoral arena (Baker 1990; Lebsock 1990). Feminist scholarship has also provided powerful critiques of scientific epistemology and methodology, pointing to the biases and limitations of scientific approaches and suggesting the need for alternative methodologies, especially methodologies that are historically and culturally specific.

The fact that scholars of women and politics have had to strive for legitimacy within academia also means that it has been difficult to concentrate on designing research useful to practitioners and activists who are working to advance women's status in American politics or improve their plight in society more generally. Most women and politics research, like academic research more generally, has been written for an academic audience. For the most part, the questions of greatest interest to academics have not been those of greatest concern to practitioners. And any results generated by academic research that might interest political practitioners have seldom reached this audience because mechanisms for communication and information dissemination have been extremely limited.

The study of women and politics stands at an important transition point. Women and politics scholarship, while still more on the margins than at the center of political science and other disciplines, has achieved a fairly secure foothold in academia. As evidence of this, the Organized Section for Women and Politics Research within the American Political Science Association currently has more than 500 members, and many scholars of women and politics have received tenure. Nevertheless, while the study of women and politics has achieved greater legitimacy, it currently faces new challenges posed by recent developments in both politics and interdisciplinary feminist scholarship.

The purpose of this volume is to help move the study of women and American politics through this transition into its next era. This volume presents a research agenda, developed by leading scholars of women and American politics, suggesting directions that could fruitfully shape the study of women and American politics in the early twenty-first century. While each chapter reviews current knowledge about a particular aspect of women's involvement in American politics, the emphasis of each chapter is on what we do not yet know, rather than on what we do know. The focus is forward, on research needs for the future, rather than backward, on what we have learned in the past.

We hope that this volume will stimulate more innovative and creative research projects employing a diversity of research methods. Certainly there is a need for research that will fill the gaps in our existing knowledge, and the various chapters of this book identify many questions that remain unanswered in existing research as well as the types of studies that are needed to address them. However, there also is a need for new research that examines the implications of recent political developments and that responds to the challenges posed by interdisciplinary feminist scholarship.

We need not only to fill in the parts that are missing in existing pictures, but also to break out of the old frames and create new pictures. Subsequent chapters will examine specific research needs on nine subjects of special interest to scholars of women and American politics: political recruitment, campaign strategy, money, political leadership, parties and women's organizations, the gender gap in voting, media, women of color, and participation outside of electoral politics. In this introductory chapter we set the stage for subsequent chapters by highlighting more general research needs and directions for research on women and American politics-needs and directions that cut across and transcend the nine subject areas. Our discussion of general research needs and directions illustrates some of the major ways in which recent developments in politics and interdisciplinary feminist scholarship have posed new challenges for scholars of women and politics.

COMPLICATING CONCEPTION OF THE CATEGORY WOMEN

Recent work in feminist scholarship has called into question the very category, "women, " which has constituted the epistemological foundation for the empirical work on women and American politics (e.g., Zerilli 1998 ; Butler 1990 ; Scott 1986 ; Young 1994). Many interdisciplinary feminist scholars, influenced by postmodern thinking, reject as essentialist the idea that all or most women share a common identity or a common set of interests, characteristics, or experiences. These scholars, who tend to be anti-foundationalist, resist totalizing generalizations and call into question the assumptions that there are underlying, discoverable truths or that people have stable, fixed identities. Rather, they see identities as fluid and provisional and believe that categories, such as the category "woman, " serve to reify one difference while erasing and obscuring other differences.

More empirically oriented scholars, trained in scientific methodology, often dismiss the writings of those influenced by postmodernism as irrelevant for their work because the anti-foundationalist assumptions that underlie postmodern thought are so fundamentally different from the Enlightenment assumptions upon which scientific work is based. Indeed, critical differences in assumptions certainly do exist. Nevertheless, we believe that postmodern feminist critiques raise important theoretical issues for empirically oriented scholars of women and American politics, especially regarding the category "women" and the way we think about gender difference. In particular, these critiques would seem to suggest that women and politics scholars should, at a minimum, be more self-conscious about the assumptions that we make in using the category and the ways in which those assumptions are structured into our research.

The use of the category "women," except when employed merely as a political strategy, is premised on the idea that certain commonalities exist among members of the category, and as scholars of women and politics we could be more self-reflective and explicit about what we assume those commonalities to be. Too often the category "women" is employed in empirical analysis without explanation as though the presumed commonalities are self-evident. Also, empirical scholars might more carefully consider whose experiences we may be downplaying or erasing in employing the category.

Postmodern feminist writings have suggested that emphasizing one type of difference, such as gender difference, necessitates the suppression or erasure of other types of differences. As empirical scholars we should be ever mindful that members of the category "women" vary in the way in which, and the extent to which, they possess whatever characteristics or experiences are assumed to constitute commonality. Much variation and diversity exist within the category; it is hardly fixed. In short, postmodern feminist critiques suggest that the category "women" may be less stable and more complicated than we have generally assumed in empirical research.

Therefore, we should perhaps be more careful and reflective in our use of the category and more explicit about the assumptions which underlie its use.

Both in the academy and in the political world outside the academy, many women of color, lesbians, and others whose work focuses on issues of diversity among women-some but not all of whom have been influenced by postmodernism-have also called the category "women" into question. They have suggested that the category "women" has generally meant "white, heterosexual, middle-class women" and that the experiences of other women have been overlooked and/or erased. Scholars have put forward various alternative models for conceptualizing the relationships among gender, race, ethnicity, sexual orientation, and class (e.g., Spelman 1988 ; King 1988 ; Collins 1990 ; Wing 1997), but increasingly theorists have opted for more complex conceptualizations that treat race, gender, and sometimes class and sexual orientation as mutually constitutive (e.g., Higginbotham 1992 ; Glenn 1992 ; Kempadoo 1999).

In this view the experiences of African American women, for example, are not simply a function of experiences they have because of their gender and experiences they have because of their race. African American women cannot separate their identities into a race component and a gender component. Rather, their experiences as African American women are uniquely shaped by a complex interplay of race and gender. Because race and gender are mutually constitutive and the effects of gender and race are analytically intertwined, African American women's experiences of gender are shaped by, and cannot be analytically separated from, their race, and their experiences as African Americans are shaped by, and cannot be separated from, their gender. The same is true for Anglo women, Anglo men, and African American men, whose race and gender are similarly analytically intertwined.

Most empirical research on women and American politics focuses on gender differences in political attitudes and behavior, examining differences between the category "women" and the category "men." Women and politics scholars have long recognized that women (and men) are not monolithic groupings and that important differences exist in the life experiences of different subgroups of women (and men). In order to account for these differences, they have usually imposed statistical controls for variables such as race, occupation, income, and age in their analyses.

This procedure assumes that gender and race, for example, are discrete categories, that their effects are analytically distinct, and that their effects can be measured separately. However, all of these assumptions are inconsistent with a theoretical perspective that views race and gender as mutually constitutive. In assuming that the effects of race are separable from the effects of gender and can be isolated and controlled for statistically, our statistical analyses are based on an understanding of the effects of race and gender that resemble what Deborah King (1988) has termed an "additive" model, in which the effects of gender are distinct from the effects of race and the effects of one are merely added to the effects of the other. This clearly is a very different understanding of the relationship between gender and race than the more complex understanding, prevalent in current feminist theorizing, of race and gender as mutually constitutive.

The critiques of the category "women" by those whose work focuses on issues of diversity among women, like the critiques by those who have been influenced by postmodern thinking, suggest that women and politics scholars need to think in more complex and critical ways about the category "women" and to consider employing alternative methods, such as intensive interviews and historical case studies, which can better reflect the complexity of the category, instead of, or in addition to, standard statistical analyses. The critiques by women of color, lesbians, and others who emphasize diversity among women also point to several other, very concrete, suggestions about future research on women and American politics. Most studies of American women and politics are based on predominantly white samples or populations of women.

Conclusions drawn about "women" based on these studies thus reflect the experiences of Anglo women to a far greater degree than they reflect the experiences of women of color. Relatively little research has explicitly and intensively examined the political orientations or behavior of women of color. (See Chapter Eight in this volume for an overview of the literature that does exist.) As a result, much more research focusing specifically on women of color is needed that takes the information we have about "women's" political involvement, based on studies of predominantly white women, and determines the ways in which the experiences of African American women, Latinas, Asian American women, and other women of color are similar to and different from those of white women and each other. Similarly, research is needed that focuses on the political involvement and experiences of lesbian and bisexual women, working-class women, women of the Christian right, and other politically significant subgroups of women whose experiences have seldom been the subject of intensive analysis.

In order to understand fully the involvement of women of color in American politics, future research projects should be devised in such a way that Anglo women's experiences are not used as the sole basis for formulating research questions. Researchers need to be sensitive to the distinctive experiences of various subgroups of women of color and to the ways in which the forms and location of their participation, the factors that motivate their involvement, and their priorities in the political arena may be very different from those of white women and from each other. In many cases new and different questions (for example, about the role of churches, participation in indigenous community groups, and immigration experiences) must be asked to understand fully the participation of women of color and their contributions to politics.

Of course, because of their life experiences and their understanding of their communities, women of color themselves may be most aware of the limitations of existing research for explaining the political participation and contributions of women of color and more likely to design studies that accurately assess the involvement and impact of women of color. The fact that there is so little research on the involvement of women of color in American politics is undoubtedly related to the fact that the vast majority of scholars conducting research on women and American politics are white.

Consequently, there is an obvious need for political science, other academic disciplines, foundations, and individual scholars and activists to encourage and facilitate the education and the research of women of color who have an interest in studying women and American politics. However, enhancing the understanding of the participation and contributions of women of color to American politics is a collective responsibility that belongs to all researchers in this field, not just to those who themselves are women of color. One of the major challenges for scholars of women and politics is to develop a base of knowledge that far better reflects the full range and multiplicity of political experiences of those encompassed by the category "women."

Feminist critiques of the category "women" have also revealed the fundamentally "gendered" nature of politics itself. Feminists have argued that political life is produced through a socially and culturally constructed system where characteristics such as rationality, strength, and political or public activity are associated with masculinity, and, by virtue of that, men. Their opposites-irrationality, weakness, and the home or private sphere activity-are quintessentially feminized and consequently associated with the "weaker sex, " women. For scholars of women and American politics this theoretical insight points to a host of unanswered research questions: In what ways are gendered assumptions and understandings written into the institutions that populate and the rules that guide the American political landscape?

How does the gendered construction of the American political system affect individual candidates, both women and men, as they run for office? How do gendered expectations about family, a woman's ability to raise money, and the like affect her decision about whether to run for office? How the gendered construction of policy does issues affect who gets assigned to particular committees and who does not?

2

Women, Elections, and Representation

WOMEN IN PUBLIC OFFICE INTELLECTUAL AND HISTORICAL BACKGROUND

Our political system did not arise in a vacuum. For Americans, its origin was in the political life of England. When the English established colonies in North America, they brought with them the concepts of local, church, and national government to which they were accustomed. Ideas of political rights and who should enjoy them were also imported from England. Thus, the English political experience is relevant to an understanding of our own system. The colonists did not simply transfer English politics to the New World, however; they adapted the familiar political forms to the different conditions of North America and to their own political views. This is where our inquiry begins: with the role of women in English and colonial political life.

The legal political role of women in colonial times was not clear at all. Political rights were based largely on birth and on property. Religion also played a part in determining who could and could not participate in politics. There was no consistent and universal barrier to the participation of women in political life, but few women voted in England and in the North American colonies, and few women participated in politics to the extent of exercising political influence. In fact, few women held any political office whatsoever in England and no women can be identified as holding elective public office in the colonies.

It was not until the period of the American Revolution that newly drafted state constitutions explicitly and completely barred women from participation in political life. In the colonial period, custom and practice were somewhat inconsistent and loose; the state constitutions, in contrast, specified political rights at the national and local level as well as at the state level. By barring women from participation in state politics, state constitutions barred women from national and local politics, as well. Thus, women were legally excluded from political life at the moment when political rights ceased to be based on custom and were instead derived from written state constitutions.

A female suffrage movement began in the early days of the new republic. In 1848, a convention for the purpose of advancing women's rights was held in Seneca Falls, New York. Among the rights advocated was the vote. What is clear from the activities and pronouncements of those advocating female suffrage, however, was that holding political office in large numbers was not a goal of the movement. For the suffragists, female political influence would derive from the vote in other ways than filling political offices with women.

Indeed, after national suffrage was granted in 1920, very few of the suffragists entered into campaigns for elective office. That simply was not envisioned by those campaigning for the vote. Strangely, political theorists, with a few significant exceptions, also have not envisioned political life in which women participate. The major exceptions are Plato, at the dawn of Western political thought, and John Stuart Mill, who lived recently enough to have participated actively in the women's suffrage movement. In the more than two millennia between these two thinkers, one can scarcely find a single major figure who imagined a workable political system such as the one we have today: a political system in which women participate equally with men.

What we found in examining the thinking of the political theorists, the historical background of our present political system, and the female suffrage movement is that with certain exceptions, the idea that women would hold public office in any large numbers was simply not contemplated or envisioned. Not until the 1950s did the idea emerge, and not until the late 1960s did such ideas receive widespread attention and support. Thus, the idea of women in public office is a relatively new one; it was not part of the political tradition of the West, it was explicitly denied as a possibility by the founders of our republic, and it was not a goal of the suffrage movement.

WOMEN AND POLITICAL REPRESENTATION

The representation of women in American political institutions is both a problem and a puzzle. It is a problem because women are poorly represented at a time when their participation in political decisions is most needed. It is a puzzle because it is not clear why women have such limited representation in our democratic institutions, nor is it clear what can be done to alter the situation. How has it come about that our democracy so effectively limits the political role of women? To answer this question, we will need to examine the period in which our nation and its political practices began. Our ideas about the place of women in American politics are often shaped by short-term knowledge of women's exclusion from the national suffrage in the nineteenth century and their fight to win it in the early twentieth. Yet, if we look back further, into the seventeenth and eighteenth centuries, we find not only that women, at some times and some places, had the right to vote, but that a few even exercised a good deal of power as political decision makers. Rather than expanding the rights exercised by a few, however, the American Revolution resulted in a denial of political rights to all women.

WOMEN AND THE FRANCHISE FROM THE 1500S TO THE 1700S

In England, and later in its American colonies, political rights, especially local political rights, were based largely on custom and usage. The right to political participation varied with place and situation. Specifications that did exist tended to be based on property, wealth, age, and religion. Although custom and usage implied that politics was for men, only occasionally was this specified in any formal way. Land ownership was considered a particularly important qualification for the franchise in a number of places in England and its American colonies.

Typically, these freeholders were male, but circumstances existed in which freehold rights could be held by women. Daughters and widows could inherit; divorced women could leave a marriage with their property; women could even be granted freeholds in their own name, and many were. 1 "By the late seventeenth century a widowed woman was listed among the top three landowners of Dedham, Massachu-setts; more than a dozen women appeared in the top tax bracket of Jamaica, New York, at the turn of the century; and as the first generation of settlers grew to maturity, the female heirs assumed the direction of sizable estates in towns throughout the colonies."

Property owners in England were typically few. Often, an English borough had only one person able to exercise the franchise and hence, to determine all local offices, including parliamentary representation. On more than one occasion, this person was a woman, even as early as the reign of Elizabeth I. Court decisions in the reign of James I both supported female parliamentary suffrage and provided evidence it was exercised.

In England's American colonies, it appears that similar conditions prevailed. A limited number of women not only had the right to the franchise but also exercised it, especially on matters relating to their property. "Recordsfrom a few Massachusetts towns show that a number of widows who owned substantial property did exercise the franchise on occasion. Moreover, the New York Gazette reported in June, 1737, that at the recent Queens County election 'two old Widdows tendred, and were admitted to vote.'"

In Rhode Island, during an era when church and village affairs were not as distinct as today, Baptist women voted in church meetings and often formed the majority. Quaker women in Rhode Island, eastern and western New Jersey, Pennsylvania, New York, Delaware, and Maryland served as ministers, participated in their own business meetings and meetings with men, served as church elders and overseers, and were selected by meetings for a variety of tasks that would be considered public today.

Even in provinces that did not permit women to vote, women may have voted or attempted to vote in local elections because practices were often at variance with the provincial law. At one point or another, some provinces, including Pennsylvania, Delaware, Virginia, Georgia, New York, and South Carolina, limited the franchise explicitly to men. At other times and in other provinces, at least some women did have the right to vote. While women in England and its American colonies were able to exercise a franchise under certain conditions in a period in which many men were not eligible, a limited number of women had the right to vote. But of those who had it, few exercised it. Colonial America was not a political golden age for women, but it did not bar them completely from political participation, either. That came about after the Revolution.

COLONIAL WOMEN AS POLITICAL DECISION MAKERS

The political involvement of women was not limited to an occasional exercise of the franchise. In England, on a number of instances between 1641 and 1649, groups of women petitioned Parliament on political issues. 10 Colonial records tell of women participating in this way as well. In 1708, a woman signed a petition concerning a local dispute in Andover, Massachusetts, and such female involvement in political petitions to legislatures was not isolated. Women could also be political figures in their own right. In 1755, Catherine Payton addressed Pennsylvania's colonial assemblymen concerning political problems faced by Quakers, and in 1741, Jane Hoskins selected and organized a slate of disaffected Quakers to contest Pennsylvania elections. We also have reports of women conducting political campaigns for their husbands in the colonial elections of Virginia, Georgia, and Pennsylvania between 1732 and 1768.

Women were prominent in a number of colonial disturbances in the period prior to the American Revolution. In 1676 in Virginia, Bacon's Rebellion broke out in reaction to the aristocratic government and political incompetence of Governor William Berkeley. Berkeley, for example, refused to allow the raising of a militia to protect Virginia against Indians, even after massacres killed over 300 colonists. A recent study indicates that women led both the Berkeleyan and Baconian camps. Among the rebels, women organized public opinion and played a leading role in their deliberations. In the American provinces, women were able to capitalize on control over property to exercise great local authority during the early period of proprietary government. In the seventeenth century, Mary and Margaret Brent were given large grants of land in Maryland. "As owners of manorial estates, they had the right to hold courts-baron, where controversies relating to manor lands were tried and tenants did fealty for their lands.

WOMEN AND POLITICS

A politician is supposed to represent others, the electorate, and not act selfishly. We know everyone will act selfishly in one way or the other, we are not angels. But there may be some ways to choose politicians that are more selfless than others. One interesting category of politicians in this respect are women. It has been know for a long time that mothers and more generous to others than fathers. This is, for example, the reason why in many countries child benefits are paid to the mother. Also, women are more risk averse, as research reviewed by Catherine Eckel and Philip Grossman shows. Also, John Lott and Lawrence Kenny show that women's suffrage in the US has coincided with more liberal policies.

A particularly interesting experiment is the requirement in India that half (correction: one third) of village council seats be reserved for women (on top of slot for various castes), and half of council heads be women. Raghabendra Chattopadhyay and Esther Duflo document that while council members follow the interests on their own gender (and caste), those headed by women tend to favor infrastructure improvements.

Why would women want to provide more public goods? Uri Gneezy, Kenneth Leonard and John List compare matrilineal and patriarchal societies, where they conducted the classic experiment designed by James Andreoni: experiment participants decide how much money to distribute between a private and a collective fund. In patriarchal societies, women share more than men. In matrilineal societies, the reverse happens. It appears thus the dominated gender is more generous.

WOMEN'S RESERVATION BILL

The real test of democracy is the creation of equality of opportunity for the hitherto deprived sections of society. It requires both a favourable social atmosphere and an individual attitude. Individual attitude and social atmosphere is a sort of reversible equation: one influences the other, in both directions. In practical terms it means that efforts have to be made at various levels of society simultaneously. Every attempt, in every direction, is bound to affect adversely some vested interests. So, one has to be prepared for a long drawn out struggle on all the fronts. Democracy in kitchen and bedroom goes hand in hand with democracy in Parliament and Panchayat. It has to become a way of life; it has to be adopted in literary vocabulary and in political discourse alike.

In the context of the present discussion it amounts to shedding of all mental reservations against reservation of seats for women in the Parliament and in Assemblies. The idea of making a legal provision for reserving seats for women in the Parliament and State Assemblies came into being during Rajeev Gandhi's tenure as the Prime Minister of India when the Panchayati Raj Act, 1992 (73rd and 74th Constitutional Amendment) came into effect granting not less then 33% reservation to women in the Panchayati Raj Institutions or local bodies. Prime Minister H.D. Deve Gowda made the actual promise for reservation of seats for women in Parliament and State Assemblies in 1996. I.K. Gujral proposed the present form and shape of the Bill during his term as the Prime Minister of India.

The Bill in its Current form envisages reserving 181 seats in the Parliament for women. In practical terms its efforts would be that 181 male members of Parliament would not be able to contest elections if the Bill is passed. Also, there is to be a rotation of seats, i.e., a male member of Parliament can not represent the same constituency for more then two consecutive terms. Here lies the rub.

These two very provisions are seemingly the cause of the consensus arrived at by various political parties to dump the Bill. 181 seats in Parliament is too great a number to be sacrificed for the mere ideal of women's empowerment or adequate political representation, the very idea makes the male politicians panicky.

The clause of 'rotation of seats' is seen by the opponents of Bill to 'strike at the very heart of democracy and democratic values' as, according to their logic, the representative will not get a chance to nurture his constituency nor the electorate will get a chance to reward or punish their representative, as a corollary to it hardly any ties would be established between the two.

This argument may hold water when it is discussed in classroom sessions but it cannot be taken as the sole basis to discard Women's Reservation Bill altogether securing 33% reservation for women in opening the doors of opportunity for political empowerment to almost 50% of our population. It will not only serve the cause of democracy as the Panchayati Raj Institutions are doing at the grassroots level but will also go a long way in ensuring political equality through active participation of woman from both urban and rural areas. Also, if social equality through political empowerment is to be achieved the, Bill should include clauses which guarantee quota within quota to women belonging to scheduled tribes, scheduled castes, other backward castes, and minority communities so that a level playing field is provided for them as well.

It is also argued that the Bill in its present form would end up ensuring seats in Parliament for the female relatives of those who are already in power. To counter this situation, provisions can be added in the Bill, which provides for no reservation to women who have close relatives in active politics (An acceptable definition of 'close relatives' can easily be arrived at.)

These women can contest from general seats. There had been suggestions in the past in the form of alternatives to the Bill. One is to amend the Representation of People's Act 1951, to compel political parties to nominate women for one-third of their seats or lose recognition. This, according to Rajindar Sachar, former Chief Justice of Delhi, is flawed, as it would violate the Constitution of India, which guarantees its citizens the right to form association under Article 19(1)(c) as a fundamental right.

Another alternative is to increase the number of seats in the Lok Sabha, which is currently based on the figures of the census of India, 1971, when the population of India was 54 crores. The numbers of seats were limited to 530 till further amendments. Now the Delimitation Commission has been asked to take the 2001 census as the basis for delimiting constituencies. According to 2001 census, the population of India has risen to 102 crores, therefore the number of seats are bound to increase before the next general elections. This should be reason enough to pave the way for the safe passage of the Women's Reservation Bill.

Moreover, when the so called backward and fundamentalist society like Pakistan can grant 33% reservation to women in its Senate then why should India, the largest democracy in the world, lag behind?

WOMEN AND ELECTIVE OFFICE: PAST, PRESENT, AND FUTURE

Where do women candidates and office holders stand in 1997, after the "year of the woman" and the "year of the angry white male"? What progress has been made toward storming the statehouses and the national legislature? What impact have women had in these positions? What advantages and disadvantages do they face? What are their goals, successes, and challenges? What are their dreams for the future?

These questions are at the heart of Women and Elective Office: Past, Present, and Future. Each assumes that having women in elective office is an important goal. Why is women's representation important? Why are we concerned about women being represented among those who make policy decisions for our government at the local, state, and national levels? As long as elected representatives are aware of and care about the interests of all their constituents, does it matter that legislatures, governors, and presidents are predominantly male?

It matters very much, for several reasons. First, a government that is democratically organized cannot be truly legitimate if all its citizens from all races and classes and both sexes do not have a potential interest in and an opportunity for serving their community and nation. Second, if all citizens are seen to have an equal opportunity to participate in the decision making that affects their lives, there is a greater likelihood that the polity will be stable and that citizens will have a reasonable degree of trust in and support for it.

Third, women constitute a large pool of talented leaders, and their abilities, points of view, and ideas can only be utilized by a society that selects its leaders from among both men and women.

It is important for women to be included among our public officials for symbolic reasons as well. If children grow up seeing women and men in the political sphere, each sex will be likely to choose from the full array of options when preparing for their adult lives. Finally, it is important for women to have full access to the public sphere because they have different life experiences from men. Because our society still operates with divisions of labor between the public and private spheres, women and men tend to have some different life experiences and points of reference. This can translate into a distinctive way of viewing existing legislative proposals and can lead to different agendas.

It is important, then, that women inhabit our legislatures and executive offices so that their concerns contribute to policy agendas.

For all these reasons, then, it matters very much that women have access to and assume elected positions. The extent to which this has been true over the course of U.S. history is explored in the following section.

HISTORY

Although women were not granted national suffrage until 1920, famous suffragist Elizabeth Cady Stanton made an unsuccessful run for Congress in 1866. Fifty years later, Jeanette Rankin of Montana became the first woman to win a congressional seat. She served twice, from 1917 to 1919 and again from 1941 to 1942. Rebecca Latimer Felton of Georgia was the first woman senator. She was appointed in 1922 and served for only one day. Ten years later, in 1932, Hattie W. Caraway of Arkansas earned the distinction of becoming the first woman elected to the Senate-or rather, reelected to a seat to which she was originally appointed. It wasn't until 1978, however, that Nancy Landon Kassebaum of Kansas became the first woman to enter the Senate by election rather than by appointment to fill an unexpired term. Nine years later, in 1987, Barbara Mikulski of Maryland became the first Democrat to do so (CAWP, 1995b; Foerstel and Foerstel, 1996).

The first women in state politics broke into political office earlier than their counterparts on the federal level. In 1895, Clara Cressingham, Carrie Clyde Holly, and Frances S. Klock all earned seats in the Colorado statehouse. Their election was due, in part, to a record number of women who went to the polls; 78 percent of eligible women voters turned out in that election compared to 56 percent of the eligible men. And, foreshadowing a pattern prevalent today, once in office, these three representatives made a priority of enacting legislation related to women, children, and families. Together, they ushered legislation through the statehouse that gave mothers equal rights to their children, raised the age of consent from 16 to 18, and created a home for delinquent girls (Cox, 1994; CAWP, 1996c).

Nellie T. Ross of Wyoming was the first female governor. She served from 1925 to 1927. To date, only thirteen women have ever served as governor: nine elected in their own right and four appointed to fill unexpired terms. The largest number to serve simultaneously was four: Joan Finney of Kansas, Ann Richards of Texas, Barbara Roberts of Oregon, and Christine Todd Whitman of New Jersey (CAWP, 1996c) all served in 1994.

Several firsts occurred only recently. In 1968, Shirley Chisholm of New York became the first African-American woman elected to the U.S. House of Representatives. In 1974, Ella Grasso of Connecticut became the first woman to win the governorship without succeeding a husband in that office (CAWP, 1996a). And a famous first was Geraldine Ferraro, who, in 1984, was the first woman to run for the vice presidency on a major party ticket.

Important firsts also occurred in this decade. In 1991, Ileana Ros-Lehtinen of Florida became the first Hispanic woman elected to the U.S. House of Representatives. In 1992, Carol Moseley-Braun of Illinois became the first African-American woman elected to the U.S. Senate. Only in 1995 did Nancy Landon Kassebaum of Kansas became the first woman to chair a major Senate committee (CAWP, 1996a; NWPC, 1995b).

All these pathbreaking victories led to an electoral situation in 1996 in which 10 percent of the U.S. Congress was female and 21 percent of state legislators were female. The most recent figures available (from March 1995) show that 18.2 percent of mayors of cities with populations over 30,000 are women (CAWP, 1995b).

At the time of this writing in November 1996, 172 women (110 Democrats and 62 Republicans) have served in the U.S. Congress. Twenty-three have been in the Senate and 149 in the House of Representatives. Of these, nineteen women of color have served in Congress. Fourteen were African-Americans, two were Asian American/Pacific Islanders, and three were Latinas (CAWP, 1995b, 1996a, and 1996b).

Women have a long history of breaking barriers to participation in the policy-making process, and in making contributions to policy. The next section explores the difficulties of that path.

WOMEN IN INDIAN POLITICS-INTERVIEWS

Margaret Alva Congress (I)

What is your personal stand on the issue of 33 percent reservation for women? I was the one who initiated this in the 80s when I was Minister for Women. It was the National Perspective Plan on Women which, for the first time, spoke of reservation from panchayats to Parliament. So right from the beginning the intention was to go right up to Parliament? That was our demand. But there was quite a lot of opposition at that time. So it was decided that we should start with the Panchayati Raj amendments and move up later. However, in 1989 the united opposition defeated the Panchayati Raj bill. We re-introduced it in 91 and it was passed. In three years the states have passed legislation as required by this constitutional amendment.

As a result, one million women have been elected to local bodies. The argument against reservation was that we will never find women who will seek election in the rural areas that they are too conservative, mostly living in purdah. However, in many states they have even exceeded the quota for example, in Karnataka, women constitute 47 per cent of the elected panchayat members. Bengal has also been a success story, as have Maharashtra, Kerala and Tamil Nadu. I am not saying that there aren't aberrations but aren't there aberrations in all the main political parties? Does every party put up saints as nominees, or even the best, most effective individuals? We need reforms not just for women the whole system of selection of candidates needs to be overhauled.

So you see reservation as part of a greater change in the system?

I believe the quality and the atmosphere of politics will improve if more women come in. I'm not saying that every one of the women who has come into the panchayat is a graduate or is appropriately qualified. But how many MPs are? How many MLAs (Members of Legislative Assemblies) are? Whenever we ask for tickets for women in the legislature they ask us are they going to win. As if every man who gets a ticket ends up as a winning candidate. Someone stated that reservation will mean admitting to the weakness of women. I say, do you have any doubts about it? After seeing the system work for 45 years, it is obvious that we are the weaker sex, whether we like it or not. We are excluded from jobs, the economic mainstream, decision-making processes, inheritance rights.

Whether one is fighting for the Scheduled Castes, the Backward Classes, or the minorities the largest group that is affected is a woman. The Khalekar report has said that women are the single largest group of backward citizens in the country. And things have not changed since then. Unless we are guaranteed an entry point by law we will never be allowed to participate. I really believe that. Some women say that we must come into decision-making positions on our own steam, but how many have come so far? To all those who say that they will do it on their own I want to ask why is the number of seats occupied by women in the legislatures declining?

You have made some personal efforts at getting larger numbers of women party tickets. What have you found to be the barriers?

We have tried but we have been ineffective because we are neither in the selection panels nor are we represented in decision-making bodies. We give lists, we fight, we recommend, but they dont listen to us. UP have 127 or so seats for the Congress, but only two women got tickets after so much talk.

I'll give you an example of a woman in Khargoda, Meerut district, who has been elected chairperson of the panchayat. She has done it on her own; the party has neither funded her nor supported her. She asked for a MLAs seat. Communally, it's a Tyagi strongh old. She is a Tyagi and an elected person. She said, dont give me any money, I will raise my own money, I dont want anything from the party, I will win you just give me the ticket. I went to the Congress president, to the members of the so-called selection committee. I went to as many people as I could. Yes, yes, her name is there, they said, her name is in the eight withheld seats, her name has been decided upon, it will be done... But in the end, what do they do? They get a man from Ghaziabad and make him the candidate in Meerut. If this is the way parties are making selections, is it any wonder that we are demanding reservation? How will the system of reservation be managed?

The election commission will reserve 33 percent of the seats by ballot for women. These are retained for women for two terms and are then rotated. In the meantime, women can establish themselves and if they are popular they will be able to contest on their own merit as general candidates by the next elections. So every constituency has a chance to throw up women. We can establish a deadline of 25 years, or five general elections, by which time the reservations for women could be withdrawn. By that time by rotation every constituency in the country would have been represented by women at least twice. This will create the nucleus for womens political leadership. What about the issue of only the wives and daughters of politicians benefiting from reservation? Maybe five to ten percent will be wives or daughters, but that does not make them any less women. The parties gave tickets to relatives of those in hawala rackets and when it comes to protecting their interests they dont mind their daughters, wives and sons contesting.

It's possible that I would not have been given an opportunity if I was not an Alva. But only those who are good enough will be able to sustain themselves. If women do not have an entry point, how will they ever get in?

How did this issue get included in your partys manifesto?

Apart from our lobbying, the importance of the womens vote forced parties to include this bill in their manifestos. The United Front government mentioned it in their Common Minimum Programme as a priority. When we raised the issue in the House, the Prim e Minister stated that the bill will be passed in the first session. The first session was coming to a close. You can see their hypocrisy they colluded to delay its introduction until the last day. This reveals their lack of seriousness on the issue.

We had argued for its early introduction so that discussions and debate could be allowed. Finally, when it was introduced, those who had never spoken about reservation for Backward Classes suddenly become the champions of Backward Class reservations. Between 1991, when the panchayat bill was introduced, until 1996 when this bill is on the ver ge of being introduced, these people did not articulate any of their concerns for the Backward Class men! The issue gains importance only now because women are about to obtain seats.

Do you think this is just party games?

No, no, even women in our party stood up to oppose the bill. There is a lobby of self-interest amongst women as well. As Narasimha Raoji said It is like a train coming onto the platform. Those who are inside dont want anyone else to get in. The greatest fear amongst male MPs is that they will lose their seats. They kept saying, Do you want to leave your seat? If you vote for this bill your seat will go. It was an attempt to create a fear psychosis amongst those seated in the house. While some parties had issued a whip, some senior MPs stood at the main gate of Parliament telling the arriving MPs, Why have you come? Go away or your seat will go. You are mad. The Minister for Parliamentary Affairs called a meeting of women MPs to discuss the bill. Once all the parties have agreed that its part of the Common Minimum Programme (CMP), why have a womens meeting? Just to create divisions of Backwards and Forwards between us? In the meeting everyone said something different; no one could agree.

What is the status now?

A Select Committee has been set up. Ive been nominated as a member of that committee. No meeting has been held yet, so we will have to see what happens. What is your position on reservations for Backward Castes? I dont want reservations for women to get mixed up with anything else. I am not proposing anything, let them fight and break their heads. Based on the Mandal Commission report we made reservations in the services. Nobody had spoken about reservation for Backward Classes or others in Parliament or legislatures. Women cut across all sections and by giving reservations to them you will be helping women from all sections to come forward. There are currently no reserved constituencies for the Backward Classes and minorities, so why should this issue get tied up with reservation for women? Are there any other measures required besides the reservation of seats? The Election Commission should announce that every party must put up a certain number of women or else they will be derecognised. Women contesting against men will be at a disadvantage so constituencies that are reserved solely for women will help them.

Uma Bharti Bhartiya Janata Party (BJP)

There are two aspects to this reservation bill: the principle of reservation and the practical application of it. In principle, I am against reservation because I believe that women should come forward on the basis of their own merit and hard work. But my 12 years of experience in politics has led me to believe that this does not happen. Large sections of people are being deprived of their human rights on account of caste and other discriminations. Women rarely manage to come forward and when they try to do so, their own colleagues brand them as loose-characters. Therefore, I believe that women will come into politics only if a reservation policy is implemented. My own entry into politics was in a large part a result of my rare luck; few women have gotten the kind of opportunities that I have. Most qualified women do not get a fair chance in politics.

Did your party ever try to encourage the involvement of women in the party?

A resolution to provide 33 percent seats in Parliament to women through a constitutional amendment was adopted by the BJP during our convention in Baroda in June 94. Advaniji, our party President, was the one who proposed it and it was passed unanimously. Ordinarily, resolutions which are put forward by party members are followed by a debate and then voted upon. However, if the all-India party President himself puts forward a proposal, it is not debated but passed directly. This is very rare in our par ty and occurs only once in 10 to 20 years. Our 1996 party manifesto states that if the BJP comes to power, we shall ensure that this constitutional amendment is made. Why didnt the BJP also resolve to provide 33 percent of the tickets to women in the party? Kalyan Singh had announced in Uttar Pradesh that in every zilla (district) at least one woman should be given a ticket. In every zilla level party meeting Kalyan Singh and Bhandari requested that at least one womans name should be put forward, but this di d not happen. This convinced me that without constitutional compulsion, men will not yield space to women. What man is willing to sit at home while his wife becomes an MLA? Will he fight for a ticket for himself or for his wife?

What are the reasons that women have not been able to come forward?

The reason is centuries old. Once the division of labour between the sexes was established, it became very difficult to change it. Woman took care of the home and men went outside to work. Men and women became physically and mentally conditioned to acc ept these separate occupations. Now all these barriers have to be broken. Most women do not have the courage to come forward without the support of a man. The society fosters the belief that women are incapable of taking their own decisions and our laws reinforce this. If a womans husband suddenly decides that there is no pla ce in his house for her, it is likely that when she tries to return to her fathers house she will find that she is not wanted there either. Because of these conditions, most women require financial, social, mental, and physical support from men.

What suggestions will you give to your party to check the tendency of politicians to give tickets only to their own female relatives?

There is a lot of opposition to nepotism in politics, especially in our party. But if people are even a little bit vigilant about this problem, tickets will have to be given to other women also. Parties will have to create a separate cell which will decide who should get a ticket. Unfortunately, what I have seen so far in the panchayat elections has not been encouraging. Women have been made the adhyaksha (head) of the Janata Parishad, Mahila Janata Parishad, Gram Panchayat, etc., but they are not doing any work. They put their thumb print down and keep their ghunghats (veils) on.

In one case I was introduced to the Janpad adhyaksha. Only after a year did I come to know that it was actually his wife who held the post! Neither he nor the public ever acknowledged his wife. Even in his speeches he addressed himself as the Janpadadh yaksha quite naturally. Since that constituency happened to have been declared reserved for women, this was how he got around this hurdle, with the endorsement of the entire constituency. Another such case is in Jatara block of Tikamgarh zilla. The people there call Surendra Singh the adhyaksha, even though it is his wife who officially holds the post. This is not uncommon. In many rural areas the husband of an elected woman automatical ly begins to act as if he is a member of the panchayat. He even manages to sit alongside her, and he keeps signalling to her what he wants her to do. Everyone knows what is going on when people have proposals they even go to the extent of contacting th e adhyakshas husband directly.

It should not be as bad at the parliamentary level as it is in the lower levels. A husband will not be able to sit alongside his wife or tell her where to put her thumb-print in the Vidhan Sabha, at least not as easily as men are doing at the panchayat level.

What is the reason that women such as Sushma Swaraj, Mamta Banerjee, Maneka Gandhi and yourself have been able to come forward and your respective parties have been unable to refuse you tickets? How difficult is it for ordinary women without familial con nections to do this?

Each one of these women has made a certain space for herself. As for myself, prior to joining the BJP, I was known as a very good orator. At first I used this talent in the religious field but then I decided that working in religious institutions alone will not remove poverty. So I brought my oratory skills, dedication, and sincerity into my political work. At the time I entered politics, apart from the Congress Party, the other parties' didnt have too much nepotism. Even the Congress had much less nepotism at the grassroot level. If someone displayed a little merit and talent they were given a chance. How ever, I still believe I was very lucky only a handful of women have the kind of luck that I did.

Is there more nepotism now?

Not really. But currently, we are having a dilemma in politics; there is lot of political uncertainty. At such a time, it is difficult to say who will gain and who will face losses.

Have you ever faced resistance in your own party while trying to promote womens advancement? Have you ever suggested the name of a woman (as deserving of a nomination) on the basis of her work, but found that she did not get a ticket?

No, this has never happened to me. But I have suggested very few names. The women whose names I have suggested for organisational work have been recruited. None of the women that I have tried to push forward have had this type of problem.

Is there a shortage of active women or are the active women simply unable to get tickets?

There is no shortage of women. Women are more capable than men, but they are unable to break the barriers. By nature, we are physically weaker than men. Earlier when humans lived in caves whoever was the strongest, physically, became the leader. In today's world, however, whoever is mentally superior should be the leader. So now women can and should be in leadership positions as well. But the old attitudes of both women and men are not changing much. Please explain the issue that you have raised regarding the need for a provision within the proposed reservation bill for Other Backward Castes, Scheduled Castes, and Scheduled Tribes. I am firm in my argument that the bill needs to be altered. We have introduced this bill because we have accepted that the weakest section of society is women. Their situation is even worse than that of Dalits.

A scheduled caste employee insulted by his employer can quit his job. However, a wife who undertakes all of the same tasks undertaken by Dalits eating jhootan (leftovers), sweeping and mopping, washing clothes, cleaning the faeces of the children, picking up shoes, etc. does not have that option.

Since I am from the Backward Castes, I know from experience that women from the oppressed classes are the weakest of the weakest section of society. She is hit twice, once outside the house because she is a Dalit and secondly, within the house because sh e is a woman. Though she shares the second type of oppression with upper caste women, she deserves some compensation for the first as well. But even after these groups got reservation in government jobs and educational institutions, there has been littl e positive change, especially among the women of these groups. I am not proposing that anyone should be given political advantage only because of their caste. Those who are promoted should, of course, be able and sincere. Those who criticise your stand on this issue say that you never brought up this issue in the past and that you are just attempting to obstruct the bills passage. I had raised this issue previously with the party and it was decided that if the BJP comes to power we will include this provision before passing the bill. As soon as Deve Gowda had become Prime Minister I communicated my stand to him through a letter.

So the BJP resolution included this clause?

No. I spoke to them later. It was decided that whenever the party introduces the Reservation bill this aspect will also be taken care of.

So do you have your partys support on this issue?

Yes, lagbhag (almost).

Do you think you will have the BJPs full support on this bill?

If one takes a secret ballot from all the men, this bill will be blown away. It will only obtain a couple of votes. Similarly there will only be about two or three votes from the Congress. However, the bill will have to be passed anyway because they want womens votes. So they will all pretend to be very happy with the bill. The other allegation is that since your party is considered to lean towards the upper castes, this issue will make the BJP look like the defender of low caste interests as well. No, this is not the case. After all, I am from the Backward Castes and I have reached a high-level post in the BJP. There are many others, also, like Kalyan Singh, Keshu Bhai Patel and Gopinath Munde. In every state, the person at the highest level is almost always from the lower castes.

Do you think that on some pretext or the other the passing of this bill will be postponed?

I have faced numerous allegations that I am at fault for stopping the passage of this bill. But I am actually a real supporter of this bill. The bill had so many lacunae that even if it had been passed it would have been debunked by the courts. I just want all the shortcomings to be removed so that we wont face any hurdles from the courts after the bills passage. No one will be able to stop this bill now. If anyone attempts to do so, the women of this country will react swiftly and strongly. There will be a new type of battle in the streets of India. Women want respect and they are demanding their share in all aspects of political and social progress.

Pramila Dandavate (JD)

Until 1975-76 I was in favour of reservation for women only up to the local and zilla parishad levels. When the Janata Dal came to power, women were given very few tickets even though they had participated in the struggle for democracy under Jaiprakash Narayan. Since then I have become a consistent supporter of reservation for women, including in Parliament. I feel that our party wants women to be decorative pieces, like achar (pickle) with food or a flower pot. They do not want to share power in the real sense of the word. I believe that unless reservations for women are constitutionally guaranteed, the number of women in these representative bodies will decline.

Womens organisations and womens wings of all political parties have concluded, on the basis of their experiences in their own parties, that men have thousands of excuses for not giving an adequate number of tickets to women. This is common across party lines. They ask so many questions - Is it guaranteed that she will win? (As if all men who contest get elected!) Will she get the required funds? Will she open her mouth? There are so many mauni babas (meditative saints) in the Parliament who never open their mouths! But when it comes to women, they ask: Will she be articulate? Will she understand? Do women have the time? Where will they come from? How will they come? They are so illiterate! The same arguments were put forward while the Panchayati Raj bill giving reservation to women was being drafted.

Reservation at the panchayat level has been a huge success. During the 1987 elections in Karnataka, 18,000 women were elected to the various local governments' bodies after the JD-led government introduced 25 percent reservation for women in the panchayats. Women proved to be better representatives than men. The government's positive experience with the women who were elected at that time influenced them to increase the reservation quota to 33 percent at the panchayat level. Subsequently, Rajiv Gandhi re alised the potential of this measure and proposed the Panchayati Raj Bill.

I think that the quality of the Parliament will definitely improve as more women come in. In the past, womens performance has been far better and they tend to be less corrupt. I won't go so far as to say that if women are elected, there won't be corruption. Not with women like Jayalalitha and Indira Gandhi who institutionalised corruption. But in general, there will be less criminalisation in politics. The women who will be elected cannot possibly be worse than the men with criminal records who current ly occupy the seats of power. Finally, if more women reach Parliament, there will be greater justice for women who are the victims of atrocities.

Is there unity amongst women MPs across party lines on this reservation issue?

All women are in favour of it. But of course, there are women who are playing their parties political game. I dont think Uma Bharti is actually against reservation but she is also a politician who wants to help boost the image of her party, despite her d ifferences with it. So she has raised the bogie of the lack of a provision for Backward Caste women.

What do you feel about a provision for Backward Castes?

We have no objection to it. However, now some parties are raising the issue of the Backward Castes for their own political gains. Everybody knows that the Panchayati Raj bill did not have any such clause. The BJP doesnt want the UF to obtain the credit for passing this bill. They are daydreaming about this government falling so they can come to power themselves. Only now that the BJP leaders have their eyes on the UP elections are they interested in letting it be known that it is their own party (and not the JD) who are so concerned about the Backward Castes. In the past, they never discussed these aspects of the bill.

What is the general reaction to this bill?

In general, men from all political parties are terribly upset because they do not know the future of their own constituencies. If 181 seats are reserved for women, many of them may lose their chance of contesting. Right now there are 36 women MPs, which means 145 more will have to come in to fill the quota if the bill passes. Though they have supported the bill publicly as a party and included it in the Common Minimum Programme, it is only now that they are realising its impact. The male members joke about the issue but basically they feel threatened. Chandrasekhar has said, what is the necessity of these 181 women? Others ask in jest: Who will make our food?

How has the issue reached this stage?

I'll give you a parallel example. While drafting the constitution, women were given equality with men. The men did not object to this at the time but later they opposed the Hindu Code Bill when it proposed to grant women equality in property rights. Even a person of the stature of Rajendra Prasad opposed the move. The same thing is being repeated now. Men included the reservation clause in their manifestos just to show how progressive they were and to obtain the votes of women. The women of the JD held the first conference demanding that the bill be introduced in the first session. We went to the leader of every political party and asked them to support it. We held state conferences as well, forcing Prime Minister Deve Gowda to go beyond lip service on the bill.

Why was the reservation lobby against a parliamentary debate?

We never objected to a debate. We only suggested that Parliament be extended or all other parliamentary business be suspended until the matter was finalised. The main objective was not to disallow a debate, but to get the bill passed in that very parliamentary session.

The men have anyway managed to stall the passing of the bill by ensuring that less than 275 members were present when a vote on the bill was called for. And now it will not be so easy to get it passed in the next session because the same men will be there with their delaying tactics. They will put up other excuses.

We accept that the bill has its drawbacks. The bill grants reservation for Lok Sabha and Vidhan Sabha, houses which have directly elected representatives. In principle, we demand reservation in the Rajya Sabha and the Vidhan Parishads as well, but it is difficult because there is no uniformity in the way those members are selected. The modus operandi will have to be decided. We wanted the bill to be passed in principle; the details can be worked out later. If the government falls, the whole process will have to start all over again. So womens organisations and women from political parties will have to take advantage of this period and work hard to ensure that a favourable public opinion is mobilised.

Do you think that qualified women are being obstructed from entering politics or are there less interest amongst women to do so?

There is definitely reluctance amongst women to participate in elections, in spite of several womens organisations demanding greater participation in the decision-making process. In my opinion, the reasons are: the lack of funding for those whose families are not willing (or able) to support them; the criminalisation of politics; rampant character assassination of women in politics; and the burden of household duties.

How will reservation tackle all these problems?

A woman whose decision has so much importance outside is gradually given recognition even within her family. Her position in the family changes due to her position outside. It is not the other way around.

What about funding?

I suggest state funding for the implementation of the bill proportionate to the performance of the party. A minimum level of funds should be made available to women candidates. Once a woman establishes a rapport with the public, financial assistance may not be required.

Are these reforms outlined in the bill? We have been demanding state funding for a long time. Criminalisation will be reduced if a greater number of women are in the fray. In addition, internship programmes to train potential women MLAs and MPs should be started by voluntary organisations as well as by government agencies. At the panchayat level they are already conducting such programmes. Is there anything that you and the other MPs can do to ensure that these things really happen? Yes, but the first thing is to see that the bill is passed. After the bill is passed in the Lok Sabha and Rajya Sabha, at least 50 percent of the legislative assemblies will also have to pass the bill using the same principle of a minimum of 50 percent at tendance and two-thirds majority of votes before it can become law.

We hope that a select committee will be set up immediately which will go into all the problematic aspects of the bill and remove the flaws. We also hope that they will come forward with their recommendations on the very first day of Parliament. Do women have difficulty setting up and nursing their constituencies, thus making it easy for the party to sideline them? Even women who have achieved something substantial in their lives and have competed favourably with men in other fields are afraid to enter the political arena. Reservation will give them exposure and training in politics. After they work in their own co nstituency for a while they will be bold enough to fight.

After each constituency has been reserved for 10 years, the reservation for that constituency should rotate. At the end of 25 years, there should be a comprehensive review, and hopefully by then we would find there is no longer any need for reservation.

So the parties have to nominate certain women to fight in these particular constituencies?

What is happening now? Even though parties are not giving women an opportunity in their own organisations, they seek women for local elections since it is a constitutional requirement because of the Panchayati Raj Act. Slowly a woman will get entrenched in her constituency and will be willing to fight in the open.

What kind of measures has your party previously taken to include a greater number of women? Or have they simply included it in their manifesto? Our party has more Backward Caste members than any other party. Backward Caste members are getting the opportunity to participate in decision-making for the first time. The men feel that it is their right, but they lack the enthusiasm for including women.

The JD constitution specifies that women must be included. Women, SCs, STs, OBCs and minorities are entitled to 60 percent of party positions. Yet women dont even constitute 30 percent. At most levels, we have at least a handful of women, but in the h igher bodies the Parliamentary Board and the Political Affairs Committee the party has not included women at all and we are fighting for that. What has been your personal experience in the party? Have you tried to obtain tickets for some women? Despite all my efforts during the UP elections, as well as before that, when I tried my level best to see that more and more women get tickets, it still has not happened. Now I am convinced that unless there is a constitutional compulsion, our men will no t give tickets to women.

What about the risk of women simply acting as pawns for the men behind them?

In the beginning, even in the rural areas, women listen to their husbands. But slowly they realise that their own opinion and their own power matters, and they begin to assert it. It depends on the socio-economic and political climate in the state. Th is is to be expected at first, but after two or three elections it will change. If the parties could put a 33 percent reservation clause in their manifestos, what prevented them from passing party resolutions to include 33 percent women candidates? You should ask this question to the party leaders.

How will the inclusion of women in Parliament alter the course of development?

A woman's perception of development is totally different from men. A male farmer will prefer a cash crop to a food crop because he wants money. However, a woman will prefer a food crop because she is afraid her husband will squander away the money. Sim ilarly, women prefer food-for-work in the employment guarantee schemes even if theres less money to be made. Men, on the other hand, prefer cash income. A number of surveys have shown that 100 percent of a womans income goes towards the welfare of the family while in the case of men a substantial proportion goes towards satisfying his whims. The priorities of women are different. We naturally think more about our families and our children. Instead of spending so much on destructive and combative activities education, child welfare, and health will become priorities. Unnecessary conflicts that are a drain on our resources will stop. Perhaps men would also become aware of this waste if they were to start looking after their families. It has to do with the fact that we have been endowed with the uterus where children are born. We are creators, not destroyers.

Vimla Ranadive (Communist Party of India (Marxist))

I feel personally that unless and until basic changes are made in our society, the major questions will not be resolved. The reason for this is the feudal nature of our society. Change depends upon the removal of these feudal tendencies. This will be a long process. Both men and women have to be convinced that change is required. For instance, this bill was sent to the select committee at the last minute. As a party we will not oppose the bill for one-third reservation even though we feel that it has its limitations. I agree that our party has a very low representation of women in Parliament and state assemblies, but I do not accept that the women in our party are in Parliament only because we are related to some male politician.

Those who are have achieved independent status. Women are doing well at the panchayat level, particularly in Bengal and Maharashtra. If you meet those women you will see that they work hard, sometimes better than their husbands do. They have also shown their ability for developing schools, encouraging literacy, etc. They are doing splendid work. They have aptitude but they should be given a chance by their counterparts to come forward.

What specific measures have you taken to encourage the participation of women?

We have started such a process in our Coordination Committee. Through our trade union we took up the issue of womens representation. We encourage membership of women in trade unions, their representation in committees, as delegates.

We sent circulars to all the states that at conferences they should ensure that there is at least 10 percent womens representation. Some states have made an attempt but two states still failed to send any women. The All-India Coordination Committee of Working Women addresses these deviations or feudal tendencies amongst trade unions. After 10 years of pursuing this issue, some changes have been made, although it is still not satisfactory. Earlier at our conferences for plantation workers of 200 to 300 delegates, there would be five or six women, even though 80-90 percent of the workers were women. As the President of the All-India Plantation Workers Union, I demanded that representation of women be increased. On the current Executive Committee of our Federation, out of 45 members, at least 20 are women. For the next conference in Assam, I have asked them to send 25 percent women. We will have to wait and see how many come.

At the party level are there any such measures being undertaken?

There are no such measures. It is a question of political consciousness. There are no women in our Politburo, which is our highest body. There are five women out of 70 members in our Central Committee. But we will not give representation to women just because they are women. We need to include women in mass-organisations such as agricultural workers associations, kisan sabhas, and student unions. If they dont come forward, they will not be able to develop themselves.

As a party how will you encourage this trend?

The Centre for India Trade Unions (CITU) and the All-India Democratic Womens Organisation (AIDWA) are both doing it. A good number of women are in the Kisan Front and they launch struggle along with the men. When I give a call for anganwadis, women are the first to come. They speak well about their own problems but they are not coming forward in the party or in the mass organisations.

Through the mass organisations we are trying to train them because they have to take up the responsibility. Are there cases of women who want to come forward but are prevented due to some weakness in the party? Yes, sometimes because of a lack of political understanding, ideological development and education, they are unable to come forward. However we are attempting to bring women into the agricultural front, the trade union front and also into the party. We are holding conferences on behalf of AIDWA, CITU and other organisations.

Have there been any individual women who could have gotten tickets but were not able to?

Yes, this happens. This is the reality and we must accept it. There will always be some women who are capable enough but are not pushed forward.

But what do you feel about the panchayat reservation? Is your stand the same or is it any different?

That will come easier, women at the grassroot level will get involved, as our experience in Bengal and Karnataka has shown. They are doing excellent work. But in the higher bodies it will be a little more difficult. Just because a woman is the wife of a politician she shouldnt get a ticket. She must also be able to contribute and speak in Parliament on behalf of women and men. What about the proposed reservation for Backward Caste members within the womens quota? I have not had a chance to study the issue so I would not like to comment.

PRIORITY FOR WOMEN POLITICIANS

Tessa Jowell, the minister for Women, warned yesterday that Labour's long-term drive to boost the number of its women MPs will be in jeopardy unless constituency parties select female candidates for the next general election.

In an interview with The Independent, Ms Jowell appealed to local parties to give priority to women in winnable seats, to prevent Labour's 101-strong band of women MPs being reduced after the election, which is expected next year.

Labour's Millbank headquarters fears the party's traditional male-dominated culture will reassert itself when constituency parties select their candidates in the next few months. Some men who failed to win seats in the Scottish Parliament and Welsh Assembly because of rules which helped women plan to take revenge by landing safe Westminster seats. "We have taken a big stride towards a more representative House of Commons," said Ms Jowell. "The message to constituency parties is: don't let us lose that progress."

Labour's target is to ensure the party has equal representation among men and women after two more general elections, and Ms Jowell says the fate of that goal now lies in the hands of party activists. "You can't talk about the importance of equality on the one hand and then do nothing about it on the other," she said.

"It is in the power of every single Labour Party member to stay true to the party's commitment to be a party for men and women."

Should local parties use positive discrimination by choosing a woman even if a more impressive man is in the running?

"Of course you make decisions on the basis of merit," Ms Jowell replied. "We have a truly outstanding panel of women putting themselves forward.

Almost all of them would give any male candidate a run for his money." Ms Jowell insisted Labour's drive was "not about tokenism or political correctness" and that a representative Parliament was one way of achieving a modern democracy. If the number of Labour women MPs fell at the next election, she accepted that a re-elected Blair government might have to change the law to allow parties to choose candidates from all-women shortlists. In the run-up to the 1997 election, an industrial tribunal ruled that such lists breached the Sex Discrimination Act.

"There are two views on how to get equal representation - by changing the law or, after getting a critical mass of women in 1997, achieving it by exhortation and changing the culture of the party," Ms Jowell said. "If we don't make progress, then I think we will have to look at changing the law after the next election."

Ms Jowell insisted Labour would do more to ensure more women MPs than the Tories, who have only 14 women MPs at present and have so far selected only 32 for the next election - many in unpromising seats. "The Tories are all mouth and no action," she said.

She conceded that the slow pace of reforming Parliament's crazy working hours was hardly an encouraging sign for prospective women MPs, but insisted Westminster's male-dominated culture was beginning to change. "Sitting through the night, hanging around, making important decisions when you have already been on your feet for 15 or 16 hours is not a good, responsible way of running the government."

She criticised last week's ruling by the Speaker, Betty Boothroyd, that women MPs should not breast-feed their babies in Commons committee rooms because non-MPs are not allowed to take "refreshment" in them. "It's absolutely breathtaking," said Ms Jowell. "What does this actually mean - that mothers with tiny babies cannot be MPs? We really have got to move into the 21st century and put some of this archaic view of the world behind us."

Ms Jowell, who is also minister for Employment and Welfare to Work, is one of an increasingly influential group of women in the Government who are persuading it to adopt more "family-friendly" policies such as better maternity and paternity rights.

Other key players include Baroness Jay of Paddington, Margaret Hodge, Dawn Primarolo and Yvette Cooper. But some critics of Tony Blair claim he has kept women in the Cabinet's backroom jobs such as leader of the Commons, (Margaret Beckett) and the Lords (Lady Jay). Ms Jowell denied the charge, saying Mr Blair would have been accused of putting them in "women's jobs" if they were responsible for health and education.

However, Ms Jowell admitted that women's concerns over health and education explained why the Government was now less popular among women than men. In 1997, Labour closed the long-standing "gender gap" which helped to keep the Tories in power for so long, but Labour's private polling suggests this might prove short-lived. "Women trust us now. But they care passionately about delivery," she said. "It is women more than men who deal day-to-day with the children's school, the clinic, the doctor, so they are impatient for change."

Ms Jowell wants to see a cultural change in the way the Government communicates with women - and believes that would also boost its appeal among men. "The tradition of politics is gladiatorial, confrontational and highly aggressive. We know that turns a lot of women off. "It turns men off too; they see politics as game-playing and point-scoring rather than delivering practical changes to make people's lives better."

She said the Government needed to talk to people in the light of their own experience and should not always use the language of confrontation. "I believe we can improve the public perception of politics in this way," she said.

Her final thought is to issue a challenge to the Blair administration: "We need to make sure the way we deliver and behave as a Government reflects the way the world now works and that we don't look like a hopelessly outdated institution that people come to visit as spectators but simply don't feel engaged with."

3

Democracy Updates

WOMEN GAIN GROUND IN BURKINA FASO ASSEMBLY

Over the past three years, Burkina Faso has seen tremendous growth in local government as a decentralization process created councils for small regions, called communes, across the country. Women, who were largely spectators in the past, now occupy 35 percent of those new seats. Now women are poised to make up at least 30 percent of candidate lists for National Assembly and loal elections, thanks in part to NDI & their work with members of parliament and civil society groups who supported the requirement. Related: Aminata Kassé, NDI's resident director in Burkina Faso, offers her perspective on the work that has been done to elevate women's role in the country as well as the challenges they still face.

WOMEN FIND STRENGTH, INFORMATION THROUGH ONLINE KNOWLEDGE NETWORK

Linking women across continents, languages and faiths is part of the success story of iKNOW Politics - an online portal through which women in politics network and share information, knowledge and expertise.

IN-COUNTRY PERSPECTIVES

Gender Quota in Burkina Faso Marks Feats Accomplished, Challenges Ahead

Aminata Kassé, a former member of the Senegal parliament, has spent the past five years working as NDI's resident director in Burkina Faso, where women's representation on local councils has risen to 35 percent across the country. Kassé discusses NDI's work in the country.

More In-Country Perspectives

Women in Politics

NDI values its collaboration with many organizations to advance the Win with Women Global Action Plan, implement programs and raise awareness about the importance of women's role as decision-makers in the political process.

UNITED NATIONS DEVELOPMENT PROGRAMME

The United Nations Development Programme (UNDP) is the development organization of the United Nations, working in over 160 countries to build local capacity and increase access to knowledge and resources. Its primary aim is to strengthen countries in their ability to achieve Millennium Development Goals.

INTER-PARLIAMENTARY UNION

Established in 1889, the IPU is the international organization of parliaments of sovereign states. It contributes to the growth and development of its member parliaments by facilitating exchanges of experience between them. The IPU also considers issues of human rights and international interest, serving as a forum for its membership to express and debate issues.

THE INTERNATIONAL INSTITUTE FOR DEMOCRACY AND ELECTORAL ASSISTANCE

The International Institute for Democracy and Electoral Assistance (International IDEA) is an intergovernmental organization, based in Stockholm, Sweden, that supports the strengthening of democratic institutions and processes around the world. International IDEA provides knowledge, expertise, and a platform for dialogue in constitution-building, electoral processes, political parties, and democracy and gender issues.

SOUTHERN AFRICAN DEVELOPMENT COMMUNITY PARLIAMENTARY FORUM

The Southern African Development Community Parliamentary Forum (SADC PF) is a regional inter parliamentary body comprised of representatives from over twelve parliaments in southern Africa. The Forum works toward the promotion of multiparty democracy, good governance, gender equality, and political stability in the region as well as respect of the rule of law, human rights and fundamental freedoms.

In this capacity, the SADC-PF organizes international observation missions to assess the elections of its member states Club de Madrid The Club de Madrid is an independent organization dedicated to strengthening democracy around the world by drawing on the unique experience and resources of its Members - 70 democratic former heads of state and government. In partnership with other organizations and governments that share its democracy-promotion goals, the Club de Madrid provides peer to peer counsel, strategic support and technical advice to leaders and institutions working toward democratic transition and consolidation.

ORGANIZATION OF AMERICAN STATES

The Organization of American States (OAS) is an intergovernmental organization comprised of 35 states from the Western Hemisphere.

The OAS works to strengthen cooperation on core democratic values defend common interests and debate the major issues facing the region and the world. Under the terms of the Inter-American Democratic Charter, OAS member states are required for holding free and fair elections, and may seek advisory assistance from the OAS to strengthen their electoral institutions and processes.

UNIFEM

UNIFEM is the women's fund at the United Nations. Established in 1976, it provides financial and technical assistance to innovative approaches aimed at fostering women's empowerment and gender equality. Today the organization's work touches the lives of women and girls in more than 100 countries. UNIFEM also helps make the voices of women heard at the United Nations - to highlight critical issues and advocate for the implementation of existing commitments made to women.

INITIATIVE FOR INCLUSIVE SECURITY

The Initiative for Inclusive Security (a project of the Hunt Alternatives Fund), including The Women Waging Peace Network, advocates for the full participation of all stakeholders, especially women, in peace processes. Creating sustainable peace is achieved best by a diverse, citizen-driven approach. Of the many sectors of society currently excluded from peace processes, none is larger-or more critical to success-than women. Through its publications, partnerships, and trainings, The Initiative has connected these women experts with over 5,000 policy shapers to collaborate on fresh, workable solutions to long-standing conflicts across the globe.

VITAL VOICES GLOBAL PARTNERSHIP

Vital Voices Global Partnership is the preeminent non-governmental organization (NGO) that identifies, trains, and empowers emerging women leaders and social entrepreneurs around the globe, enabling them to create a better world for us all. We provide these women with the capacity, connections, and credibility they need to unlock their leadership potential.

CEDPA

Founded in 1975, the Centre for Development and Population Activities (CEDPA) is an internationally recognized non-profit organization that improves the lives of women and girls in developing countries. Our approach is to work hand-in-hand with women leaders, local partners, and national and international organizations to give women the tools they need to improve their lives, families and communities.

THE COUNCIL OF WOMEN WORLD LEADERS

The Council of Women World Leaders is a network of current and former women presidents and prime ministers. The Council's mission is to mobilize the highest-level women leaders globally for collective action on issues of critical importance to women and equitable development. By increasing the number, effectiveness, and visibility of women who lead at the highest levels in their countries, the Council aims to promote good governance and enhance the experience of democracy globally.

INTERNATIONAL REPUBLICAN INSTITUTE (IRI)

A nonprofit, nonpartisan organization, the International Republican Institute (IRI) advances freedom and democracy worldwide by developing political parties, civic institutions, open elections, good governance and the rule of law.

WOMEN'S ENVIRONMENT AND DEVELOPMENT ORGANIZATION (WEDO)

Founded in 1991 by Bella Abzug and Mim Kelber, the Women's Environment & Development Organization (WEDO) is an international organization that advocates for women's equality in global policy. Working in key global forums such as the UN, WEDO advocates for and seeks to empower women as decision makers to achieve economic, social and gender justice, a healthy, peaceful planet and human rights for all.

THE WOMEN'S FOREIGN POLICY GROUP (WFPG)

The Women's Foreign Policy Group (WFPG) is a non-partisan, non-profit, educational membership organization that promotes global engagement and the leadership, visibility and participation of women in international affairs. The WFPG's in-depth global issues programs feature women leaders and highlight their contributions and voices. The organization also hosts leadership development activities to promote the next generation of women leaders.

FEWER WOMEN THAN MEN RUN FOR PUBLIC OFFICE

In 1994, the National Women's Political Caucus issued a report on the success rates of male and female candidates. Its conclusion: "When women run for office, they win as often as men do."

Jody Newman, the report's author, compiled a massive data base of more than 50,000 candidates to look at the experiences of men and women in state legislative, congressional and gubernatorial contests. The challenge, according to Newman, was getting more women to run.

Fast forward 14 years to a new report, "Why Are Women Still Not Running for Public Office?" from the Brookings Governance Studies program. Written by Jennifer L. Lawless and Richard L. Fox, the May 2008 report examines the attitudes of professional men and women lawyers, business people, educators and activists about running for office. The researchers interviewed 3,700 professionals in 2001 as part of the Citizen Political Ambition Study and re-interviewed around 2,000 of them in 2008. They found a persistent gender gap in political ambition.

Women have been making slow progress

In the report, 56 percent of the professional men, compared with 42 percent of the women, had ever considered running for political office. The women in the survey were slightly more likely than the men to have thought about running for local office, such as the school board (39 percent to 33 percent), but for the offices of state legislator, governor, House representative or senator, the men were more interested.

The professional women in the survey felt more negatively about the mechanics of running for office, including having to raise campaign cash or possibly having to go negative in a campaign, than men did. Loss of family time and privacy were greater deterrents for the women than the men.

In the survey, fewer women than men said a party or elected official had ever suggested they run. The researchers also pointed to women's greater familial responsibilities as possibly holding them back. Finally, these professional women thought themselves less qualified than the men to run (55 percent to 70 percent).

For the report's authors, women's underrepresentation in our politics raises "grave concerns over the quality of democratic governance and political legitimacy." I don't see it that way.

One impression I took away from the survey was that a political career is not very attractive to either men or women. Although the professional men were almost twice as likely as women to display interest in any federal position, only a quarter of men and 13 percent of women had considered it. Lawless and Fox say that researchers agree that there is a "complete absence of overt gender bias" in fundraising and vote totals. Today, women have myriad choices and interests, and they can make contributions in many ways. While they may cheer the success of Hillary Clinton, Sarah Palin and Nancy Pelosi, it's not clear how many of them would make the choices they have made. Nor do I believe that only women can represent women's views or experiences. Women aren't a monolith politically.

There are 16 women in the Senate today, a number that could rise to 17 next month. One hundred and thirty-three women are running for House seats, not a banner year. Women have been making slow progress because our political system favors incumbents. As Newman said in her study, "winning elections has nothing to do with the sex of the candidate, and everything to do with incumbency." Most incumbents are men, and incumbents enjoy a huge advantage. When these seats open up, women will win them just as often as men. Until that happens, women's overall representation will be low.

WOMEN IN KENYAN POLITICS

Kenyan women have truly come a long way in penetrating through the political male-dominated world. Kenya's political history has recorded great women who went through many difficult and humiliating conditions to fight for equality and participation in politics. Some of these difficulties include the beating of female candidates by the supporters of rival male candidates, male power play (manipulating and possibly rigging women out) and the lack of funds for women politicians. Since Kenya's independence from the British rule in 1963, female representation in Parliament has been very low. During the last Kanu (Kenya African National Union) regime that ended in 2002, there were only nine women out of the 220 members of parliament (MPs). There has also been very low female representation in decision-making positions within government sectors/departments, the local government (municipalities) and parastatals.

In the current Narc (National Alliance of the Rainbow Coalition) government, the number of female MPs has at least increased to 18 out of the 222 members of parliament. However, this still falls short of the United Nations target of achieving 30% representation of women in politics.

It also falls short of the Beijing Platform for Action (the Fourth World Conference for Women in 1995), where it was agreed by all governments that there should be equal participation of women and men in decision-making bodies. The gender imbalance in Kenya's political playing field has widened so much, since the male political ideology continues to define the standards of evaluation of women's political performance and participation.

Women MPs continue to play second fiddle and none chairs a parliamentary committee during this ninth Parliament. They are even still not allowed to carry handbags into the House, according to the archaic male-dominated colonial rules.

What hinders women from being frontrunners in politics?

One of the major problems that women face is the lack of funds to conduct elections. Due to the feminization of poverty, many women interested in politics are faced with financial constraints which bar them from contesting, compared to their male counterparts; hence their political potentials go unnoticed.

The political parties' structures are also male-dominated, thus are discriminative against women. It therefore becomes challenging for women to voice themselves or to take leading positions. Most of these parties only nominate men to winnable positions during elections. It is also evident that very few women politicians are seen hitting the campaign trails. If present, they are rarely heard on the podium because the campaign rallies are often male-dominated. It is paradoxical that women form the majority of Kenyan voters.

Certain cultural aspects also block women, who are portrayed as not possessing strong leadership qualities; many Kenyan communities still believe that men should lead. Combining politics and 'child-rearing'/family life has also proved to be challenging. For many women, it is hard to balance both private and public life, which in most cases have interfered with many marriages.

Media coverage on the successes of women politicians and potential contenders is limited compared to their male counterparts.

What to do?

The success of women in politics in Rwanda, Liberia, Sweden and South Africa for example, shows that there are many strategies women can use to gain power. Women in Kenya should feel challenged and call for affirmative action to increase their participation in decision-making bodies. They should unite and actively participate in nation-building activities.

Which is the best party for women to voice themselves?

Of all the strong and main political parties present in Kenya, only Narc-Kenya seems to be women friendly. Narc-Kenya, unlike ODM-K (Orange Democratic Movement of Kenya) seems to have an upper hand when it comes to addressing gender issues. The party does not only have a larger number of women representatives, but its policies are also gender sensitive and the party seems ready for affirmative action. It is the first party to hold a rotational national party chairmanship, giving all a chance to lead, including women. President Kibaki has also advised public institutions to increase female participation in key positions. ODM-K on the other hand, is spearheaded by male chauvinists who are not gender sensitive and are about to get rid of Nazlin Umar, one of their two female presidential candidates.

It is time for women to look for a way forward and join Narc-Kenya, the party which they can approach to air their grievances and allow them to participate fully in politics.

CRIMINALITY, NOT PATRIARCHY, DETERS WOMEN IN POLITICS IN INDIA

With only a fraction of women candidates contesting the ongoing parliamentary election, political empowerment of women is a far cry. The factors that prevent women from stepping into a territory where criminals and corrupt politicians rule the roost.

"Crime and corruption are bigger deterrents to the entry of women into politics than patriarchal attitudes or any other factor," Madhu Kishwar, founder of *Manushi Sangathan*, an organisation that works for women's rights, told in an interview.

Before the start of the ongoing elections, staggered in five stages between April 16 and May 13 to accommodate some 715 million voters, major parties pledged once again in their manifestos to usher in what they have glaringly failed to do since 1997 – arrive at a consensus on legislation to reserve 33% of seats in the Lok Sabha (Lower House of Parliament) and in the state assemblies for women.

A measure of poor progress in female participation can be had from the fact that 44 women were elected to parliament in the last general elections held in 2004 – the exact same number as in the 1984 elections conducted 20 years ago. Of the 6,538 candidates in the first four stages of the ongoing elections only 462 are women.

An easier route to political power for women is to ride on the success of male relatives and gain visibility and power within political parties before attempting to win parliamentary seats by taking to the gruelling campaign trail.

"For the ordinary woman who aspires to be a candidate the odds are nearly insurmountable"

Take Sonia Gandhi who owes her pre-eminent position in Indian politics to her membership of the dynastic Nehru-Gandhi family that enjoys unquestioned control over the ruling Congress party.

Similarly Mayawati, currently chief minister of India's largest province of northern Uttar Pradesh, owes much of her success to her late mentor and companion Kanshi Ram who mobilised India's dalits into a formidable political force under the banner of the Bahujan Samaj Party.

Jayaraman Jayalalithaa, who served twice as chief minister of Tamil Nadu, was brought into politics by the late M.G. Ramachandran, her constant companion and co-star in many blockbuster Tamil movies of the 1960s and 1970s.

Jayalalithaa, like Mayawati, is considered prime ministerial material. "Such women rarely encourage other women to come up within their parties," said Ranjana Kumari, president of Women Power Connect, an umbrella for some 700 women's organisations and individuals.

"For the ordinary woman who aspires to be a candidate in an Indian general election the odds are nearly insurmountable," Kumari said, adding that on top of everything else female candidates have to contend with criminalisation of politics.

"Because the current election is one of the most closely fought between the Congress party and its allies in the United Progressive Alliance coalition and its rivals in the Bharatiya Janata Party (BJP) - led National Democratic Alliance, the 'winnability' of each candidate is critical, and that means calling into play money and muscle - areas that are often linked to criminality," Kumari explained.

Contesting a parliamentary seat calls for the raising of, on average, around two million US dollars - all of it in cash since the taxation system makes it nearly impossible to fund a candidate or a party legitimately.

"Politics is dirty, and, if you are a woman, you may need the support of male family members, a father, brother or a husband to act as a buffer against the payoffs, the land-grabbing, extortion and underhand dealings," said Kishwar.

Indeed India's vast 'black (or parallel) economy' is closely linked to its electoral system with one feeding on the other. "Over the last 15 years there has certainly been a tendency for more candidates with criminal charges against them to be standing for the elections," says Sanjay Kumar, deputy director of Lokniti - a programme for comparative democracy.

Kumar, an expert on electoral mobilisation and electoral violence, said that while women may not decline an opportunity to contest a seat merely for lack of money or muscle power, political parties do not have sufficient confidence in their 'winnability' in the face of these factors.

In its manifesto, the Congress party claims credit for having successfully steered Constitutional amendments through parliament in 1993 to reserve 33% of seats in the village panchayats and urban local bodies for women.

"Today, about 40% of the elected representatives in panchayats are women, compared to a reservation of 33% mandated for them. This is nothing short of a quiet revolution," the Congress manifesto crows, vowing to extend the quota to the national and provincial legislatures if voted back to power. However, the Congress party's arch rival, the BJP, has in its manifesto accused the Congress party of "not having the courage to stand up to its allies who are opposed to the political empowerment of women".

"The best way for women to contribute is to get more involved in local level politics where they already enjoy reservation"

But both the Congress party and the BJP are fielding fewer women candidates this time than they did in the 2004 elections.

Kishwar comments that the best way for women to contribute, at this stage, is to get more involved in local level politics where they already enjoy reservation, "because it is easier to begin cleansing politics of crime and corruption at the neighbourhood level".

Also, until reservations are extended to parliament and the state legislatures women should push their parties into democratising internally and giving competent women a chance to get nominations on the basis of merit rather than family ties," Kishwar said.

MAURITIUS: WHERE ARE THE WOMEN POLITICIANS

Mauritius has the lowest representation of women in government and parliament in the Southern African Development Community (SADC). But there is hope, says the only female minister in the Port Louis cabinet. "Mauritius' government is gender sensitive and it has the potential to improve the percentage of women in government and parliament in next year's elections", says Arianne Navarre-Marie, the Mauritian Minister of Women's Rights.

Of the 70 members in parliament only four are women. Navarre-Marie is the only woman in a cabinet of 25 ministers. Mauritius has a population of 1.2 million-51 percent are women. Navarre-Marie says women are partly to blame for the low representation. They do not participate in politics because they fear they might have to sacrifice their family lives and careers.

Navarre-Marie and Mauritian media practitioners attending the first southern African Gender and Media Summit that started in Johannesburg on Sunday said the coalition system hampered the participation of women in the Indian Ocean Island. And, they say, Mauritius is a patriarchal society. "There are many factors that are obstacles to women's participation in politics in my country," says Navarre-Marie. "We are a patriarchal society and even though women are equal in education, there is an attitude which prevents us from participating in politics. We can be pilots, judges, doctors, etc but when it comes to participating in politics women normally hesitate. We are not ready to sacrifice our careers and families.

Navarre-Marie who joined politics at the age of 20 in 1982, says her political commitments have prevented her from spending enough time with her two children. "Thank goodness I have a husband who has some time for my children, but for whom I would not have been able to pursue a career of my dreams. I have had ups and downs, which many women are not prepared to face," says Navarre-Marie.

Loga Virahsawmy, a veteran journalist and the president of Media Watch Organisation in Mauritius, says Mauritius boasts of being a democratic country but its statistics show otherwise in terms of women's involvement in decision-making. She says men in politics were never prepared to make room for women. "Mauritius is a very hierarchical and patriarchal society," she says. "It is a complex society in terms of religion and culture. All ethnic groups want to be covered in Parliament but they do not want women to represent them."

She believes the solution lies in a quota system in accordance with the SADC principles that call for 30 percent women in all decision-making political structures. "But the media has to do a lot of lobbying ahead of the 2005 elections; otherwise it will remain a dream and a pledge."

Jean Claude de L'Estrac, the editor in Chief of La Sentinelle media group, Mauritius' largest media group, says despite having few females in parliament and only one in the cabinet, Port Louis is a gender sensitive government with progressive laws concerning women, including the Domestic Violence Act and the Sexual Discrimination Act. "The government has done a lot for both women and children in the last 20 years. For example, an office of the ombudsperson for children has been introduced and Sherin Aumeerdy, a former minister for women's rights, will head it," says de L'Estrac.

De l'Estrac, a former cabinet minister, says the number of women in politics was likely to increase from next year because of constitutional reforms taking place in their country. On why there are few women in politics in Mauritius, de L'Estrac says: "That is not done on purpose-previous governments had many female ministers and MPs, though not an equal number with males. The country's governments are usually coalitions and women tend to become the victims. When two political parties fuse, few politicians are sacrificed. These sacrifices must be gender balanced – let's have both male and female politicians affected equally."

De L'Estrac says proportional representation may be introduced before the 2005 elections, which will probably take place in May. "With some form of proportional representation likely to come by the time we have the next election; more women are likely to be in parliament and in government. The feasibility and practicability of that will have to be tested. We have competent female politicians but the issue of political will is the main factor and we have to wait and see."

WHY POLITICIANS LOVE GIMMICKRY?

It may not fetch them the votes, but politicians often resort to gimmickry to attract attention and enhance their popularity.

When seven women politicians posed naked for a political campaign in Poland, it was dismissed as political gimmickry. Their message: "We are beautiful, nude and proud." In fact, they triggered a worldwide debate, whether political gimmickry is worth it. Now, it remains to be seen if this stunt will fetch them votes and seats in the Polish Parliament.

Politicians love gimmickry. The uncrowned Queen of Gimmickry in India is Uma Bharati, the Bharatiya Jan Shakti party leader. Recently, she created a flutter in Indore by walking into a Reliance Fresh outlet, dressed as a sabziwalli, with a basket of vegetables on her head and tomatoes in her hands as her weapon.

While Union railway minister Laloo Prasad Yadav decided to increase his popularity by being a judge on a musical talent hunt show, most political figures use gimmickry to enhance their grassroots standing. In fact, Vijay Goel, a BJP leader, has Bollywood stars like Poonam Dhillon, Suresh Oberoi, Smriti Irani and Mukesh Khanna making an appearance at his election campaigns. Known for his sharp political skills, Goel has been dubbed by his detractors as 'master of political gimmickry'. Says Goel, "I don't think bringing Bollywood stars to campaign is gimmickry. It helps me communicate my views to the public. Let me tell you, people can't be fooled. Gimmickry can't take you too far. The stars can't get anyone votes, they just help get attention."

Political gimmickry is all about attention and getting heard. There are times when political gimmickry can become a potential problem. *TIME* magazine reported how former US President Jimmy Carter relied too much on his style. Political imagery is important for a politician, says Sushil Kumar Modi, deputy chief minister of Bihar. "Bihar is known for political gimmickry all because of Laloo's image and style. He's got a casual manner of talking. Right from his university days, Laloo was an expert at dramatics and humour."

Can political gimmickry ever have a backlash? "Sometimes," says Mehbooba Mufti, PDP MP, "I really don't think political gimmickry should be encouraged. Politicians sometimes accuse each other's genuine efforts as gimmickry also. To me, Lalooji isn't a gimmick. He's done a lot of good work too for the grassroots. In governance, politicians use gimmickry to showcase themselves and their work. In this celebrity-starved culture, politicians bring Bollywood stars to woo voters. But people are smart, they come, sing and dance, but vote for who they feel is sincere. So, all the tamasha and gimmickry won't get you the votes. Sometimes, political gimmickry helps touch an emotional chord, but politicians will need to follow it up with action."

In fact, gimmicks are all stars of clever riposte, they know how to use a political situation to their advantage. Says image consultant Dilip Cherian, "Gimmickry can work for individuals but not for political parties. There have been politicians who go on dharnas, give speeches, but it may not help their party.

That's when gimmickry becomes just a stunt to get attention."

That's something Sukhdev Singh Dhindsa, MP, (Shiromani Akali Dal) agrees, "During my life, I've seen so many political games and gimmicks. In smaller towns of India, politicians use gimmickry to become popular. In Punjab, where I've seen heroes being born, political games are common and so is gimmickry." For instance, Dera Sacha Sauda chief, Gurmit Ram Rahim Singh, stirred many controversies in Punjab by wearing clothes like Guru Gobind Singh, but later apologised for dressing like the guru.

Why does everyone call Lalooji, the finest master of political gimmickry in India? "It's the perception about him," says Shivanand Tewari, national spokesperson for Janata Dal, "Lalooji used gimmickry from the very beginning, when he was in university. He became popular through a play titled Lahur Singh, aired on All India Radio in those days. Laloo spoke the dialogues very well. The stories about him are endless. When he was in jail, he distributed toffees to the kids and told them 'Go and shout slogans, Laloo will be free'. They did. Gimmickry has been his strength and downfall. Politics won't be politics without gimmickry."

WOMEN POLITICIANS OR PSEUDO MEN?

"In the Arab world today, the issue of women's rights has become something of a political football. It is not just a matter of modernity versus traditionalism, or secular versus Islamist; the issue, as so many others, has become one of the Arab worlds versus the West."

A friend of mine, an American woman very active in advocating for the Palestinian cause, met the late President Yasser Arafat not long before he was taken to Paris on his last journey.

Arafat was always very sympathetic toward women's causes. It is well known that no one representing women's rights organizations would ever leave a meeting with Abu Ammar empty handed. It was perhaps therefore especially poignant that before my friend left him, he confided in her his two greatest fears for the future should he die. One was what would happen to religious pluralism. The other was the issue of women's rights.

In the Arab world today, the issue of women's rights has become something of a political football. It is not just a matter of modernity versus traditionalism, or secular versus Islamist; the issue, as so many others, has become one of the Arab worlds versus the West.

This is extremely unfortunate. The issue of women's rights is one of equality, not emulation, whether emulation of the West or emulation of men. But perhaps it would be useful to look at the experience of our sisters in the West to see what could be used and what should be avoided.

Back in the 1960s, female politicians in the West were focused very much on women's rights. This is no longer the case. Instead, women politicians behave more and more like pseudo men. Two examples spring readily to mind. In Britain, Margaret Thatcher very ably beat men at their own game to become prime minister and earn the reputation as an Iron Lady. In the United States today, Hillary Clinton is the most prominent female politician, and one often spoken of as a potential future president. She has become so by playing a male game better than her male competitors.

But if women are to enter politics merely to do what men do, the question is, why bothered? After all, it would not be an exaggeration to say that the course of history was charted by men playing men's games by men's rules. Men's tendency to resolve conflict with violence is what has led to the frequency of war, the building of many walls and the state of the world today.

There are many women in politics today. There are a fair number of women in Arab parliaments, the Palestinian Legislative Council a notable example. But the presence of women in the halls of power is not sufficient. That is mere tokenism. What matters is the effect of that presence.

I don't want to pay flippant lip service to feminism. When we talk about equality we must talk about equality of opportunity rather than equivalence. The real reason women should be engaged in politics at all levels is not to emulate men but to bring a unique feminine weltanschauung to bear on the decision-making process. This has never been tried. The only example I can think of where exclusively female action led to political change comes from literature. In Aristophanes' Lysistrata, the women, exasperated by their men's unwillingness to resolve an age-old conflict, decided to withhold matrimonial privileges until the menfolk agreed to end their conflict. Not surprisingly, it worked.

Arab women are several steps behind their sisters in the West with regards to claiming their rights. Insofar as it forces Arab women to focus on the issue of what their rights are, this is not a bad thing. That loss of focus in the West has led to confusion. Equal rights mean being able to bring your own perspective to bear. It does not mean doing what men do, and how they do it.

And if ever there was a time when a new perspective and a new weltanshauung was needed in politics, whether in the Middle East or globally, it surely is now.

4

Women's Marginal Role in Politics

The law to reserve one-third of the total number of seats for women was implemented at the panchayat and zilla parishad level in all the states of India without any opposition from any political quarter whatsoever. Ramakrishna Hegde's government in Karnataka started this process in 1983 before the central legislation mandating representation for women was passed. It provided for 25 percent reservation for women at village panchayat levels.

This was before any powerful women's lobby emerged in Karnataka to press for this move and before there was any popular groundswell of opinion in favour of women's reservation. In the mid 1980s, the Shetkari Sangathana of Maharashtra, led by Sharad Joshi, pioneered the move to field all-women panels for panchayat elections in that state and subsequently focused on getting women elected to zilla parishads in as many constituencies as possible, with men of the Sangathana playing a supportive role.

However, the Bill introduced in the Parliament in Septemeber 1996 to reserve one-third of the seats in Parliament and state legislatures has evoked a good deal of resistance and opposition. This despite the fact that all our major national parties - the Congress, the BJP, the Janata Dal, and even the two Communist parties have committed themselves to reserving 33 percent of the seats in legislatures for women by including this promise in their respective election manifestos. The Common Minimum Programme (CMP) agreed upon by the various parties constituting the present UF government starts its section entitled "Social Justice" with the declaration that "one-third of the elected membership in Parliament and state legislatures will be reserved for women.

Legislation, including an amendment to the Constitution, if necessary, will be introduced to reserve one-third of all posts in government for women.... All laws will be reviewed to remove provisions which discriminate against women." Though they dare not openly backtrack from their promise, it is evident that they did not expect to be called to account so soon and so earnestly. News reports indicate that the greatest opposition to this bill is coming from the United Front MPs. Some of them have openly declared their intention to even defy the party whip (if one is issued) and vote against the bill.

Compare the present day controversy over the issue of women's representation in legislatures to the atmosphere that prevailed in the 1920s. In response to the Indian agitation for representative government, the British government set up a committee headed by Montague and Chelmsford in 1919 to work out a proposal for constitutional reforms aiming at the inclusion of some Indians in government. Many groups presented their case for representation before the committee.

Among the many delegations that met this committee, Sarojini Naidu and Margaret Cousins led a small delegation of women to demand that women be granted the same rights of representation in legislatures as men. The British government predictably thought this demand was quite preposterous because women in most Western countries had still not been given the right to vote, despite a protracted struggle. The Southborough Committee stated that "the extension of the vote to women would be premature in a society which continued to enforce purdah and prohibitions against female education."

However, instead of taking on themselves the onus of rejecting the demand outright, the British government simply skirted the issue by leaving it up to each of the individual provincial legislatures that they had just set up in India to grant or to refuse the franchise to women.

Their assumption was that since Indians were so "backward", they would never accept the idea of equal political rights for women. But despite the fact that at this time there was no mass-based women's suffrage movement in India, each of the Indian provincial legislatures voted to make it possible within a short span of time for women to be represented at par with men without much fuss.

The testimony of Margaret Cousins, an Irish feminist who played a major role in women's organisations in India as well as in Britain, brings out the contrast between the Western and Indian response to women's political rights very clearly. "Perhaps only women like myself who had suffered from the cruelties, the injustices of men politicians, the man-controlled press, the man in the street, in England and Ireland while we waged our militant campaign for eight years there after all peaceful and constitutional means had been tried for fifty previous years, could fully appreciate the wisdom, nobility and the passing of fundamental tests in self-government of these Indian legislators....

Between the Madras Legislative Council in 1921 and Bihar Council in 1929 all the legislative areas of India had conferred the symbol and instrument of equal citizenship with men on women who possessed equal qualifications - a certain amount of literacy, property, age, payment of taxes, and length of residence."

These limitations were included solely because the British were only prepared for limited suffrage for those who possessed a certain amount of property and education. They were not willing to consider universal adult suffrage. When a meeting of representative women's organisations in 1930 drafted a memorandum demanding immediate acceptance of adult franchise without gender discrimination, it was turned down by the British government. The same demand received a totally different response from the Indian leaders. The very next year, in 1931, the Karachi session of the Indian National Congress took the historic decision committing itself to the political equality of women, regardless of their status and qualifications. This proposal met with virtually no opposition.

Laws claiming to protect women's rights have seldom evoked the same amount of hostility or opposition in India that they provoke in many other countries of the world and get to be easily endorsed by the entire political spectrum. In fact, in India there is very little difference between parties of the right or left on women's issues. For instance, the BJP's current manifesto sounds even more progressive than the left parties on women's issues.

It took women in Europe a century-long struggle to win the right to vote. By contrast, the right to vote and other legal rights came without a fuss or fight in India. The right to abortion, right to equal employment and educational opportunities, equal remuneration for equal work, protection against domestic violence - all came to be passed as laws in India without any hostility or resistance. However, since our government neither has the political will nor the appropriate machinery to implement any of its laws (not just those relating to women but even traffic laws) little of our progressive legislation makes an impact on citizens' lives.

People's Response Our country has had a well-entrenched tradition whereby a party, politician or public figure bad-mouthing women in public or opposing moves for women's empowerment are strongly disapproved of and usually rejected. As far as I can remember, among our male politicians, only Bal Thackeray of the Shiv Sena had the stupidity to make some brazenly anti-women statements some years ago. In the assembly elections that followed, his party suffered a major setback in Maharashtra, which was attributed to his indiscreet anti-women remarks, among other things. Because of this, very few politicians dare attack women from public platforms except when they are in direct electoral competition with a woman.

This is not just due to the pressure on our politicians to be "politically correct" on women's issues. Indira Gandhi as the first woman Prime Minister of India was rarely attacked on account of her gender. If anything, she was able to use her gneder to her advantage projecting herself as Mother India and Durga incarnate rolled into one.

There was no fuss made over her assuming the highest political office in the land. By contrast, many of the supposed advanced democracies of the West are still not ready for women in such high offices. The first woman prime Minister of France was constantly derided and attacked for being a woman till she simply resigned from the job. There is indeed a widespread social opinion in favour of women's active political participation.

The recent countrywide post-election opinion survey conducted by the Centre for the Study of Developing Societies for India Today provides the most encouraging and definitive endorsement that there is no real divide between men and women in India on this issue. 75 percent of men and 79 percent of women favour active participation of women in politics and 75 percent of men and an equal number of women favour reservations for women in legislatures.

On the eve of assembly elections in Uttar Pradesh, I interviewed scores of men and women in Meerut constituency to gauge people's response on a range of political issues, including reservations for women. Barring one Sikh couple, everyone I interviewed expressed strong feelings in favour of reservations for women. This included men and women from supposedly conservative Muslim families, illiterate working-class Hindus and Muslims, and representatives of the Balmiki and Jatav (sweeper) communities, apart from the middle and upper classes. Men and women alike said that the inclusion of women was both necessary and desirable and would be beneficial not just for women but for politics as a whole.

Table 4.1: Percent of Parliamentary Seats in the Lower House Occupied by Women in Selected Countries, 1994 (Source: The World's Women 1995: Trends and Statistics. United Nations, New York, 1995.)

Australia	9
Austria	21
Bangladesh	10
Belgium	9
Chile	8
Czech Republic	10
Denmark	33
Finland	39
France	6
Germany	21
India	7
Japan	3
Mexico	8
Netherlands	31
New Zealand	21
Norway	39
Poland	13
Russian Federation	10
Sweden	34
Thailand	4
Turkey	2
UK	9
USA	Senate 9 House of Representatives 11

Despite all this, women have been politically marginalised in our country and most of them live extremely restricted lives. They are not allowed to have much of a voice even within their own community's decision making processes, leave alone having a meaningful say in national politics. In addition, today we are witnessing a serious backlash. Not just politicians but even many intellectuals are angrily rejecting the idea of reservations for women and calling it a retrogressive move.

Peripheral Role of Women Most countries in the world have failed to give due space and representation to women in political institutions. Even in societies where women exercise relatively more freedom in day-to-day living, they remain politically marginalised. As one can be seen in Table 4.1, women have done extremely well in the Scandinavian countries- Sweden, Norway, Denmark, and Finland, where they are moving in the direction of near equal participation. In these societies women have begun to seriously alter the very nature of politics and have made enduring and substantial gains for themselves in every field. In India, the problem is more serious because while in many other countries women are inching forward bit by bit, in India the participation of women in politics is actually declining. There were many more outstanding women leaders and workers in the Congress Party at all levels during the freedom movement than are present today in all the parties put together. Table 4.2 shows women's declining representation in the legislatures of a few select states and Table 4. 3 show the stagnant representation of women in the Lok Sabha since Independence.

Table 4.2: Representation of Women and Men in State Legislatures (Source: A Status Report on Participation of Women in Panchayati Raj. Institute of Social Sciences, New Delhi 1995.)

States/UTs	Year	Total	Women	Year	Total Women	
Andhra Pradesh	1957	252	11	1994	294	9
Karnataka	1957	179	18	1994	224	7
Kerala	1957	127	6	1991	140	8
Madhya Pradesh	1957	218	26	1993	320	12
Punjab	1957	101	5	1992	117	6
Rajasthan	1957	136	9	1994	200	9
Tripura	1957	30	0	1992	60	2
Uttar Pradesh	1957	341	24	1993	425	12
West Bengal	1957	195	11	1991	294	18
Delhi	1972	56	3	1993	70	3

Puzzling Contradictions One of the most puzzling features of low political representation of women in our legislative bodies is that it seems to have no direct correlation with literacy and other seemingly logical indicators. A comparison between the states of Kerala and Rajasthan, whose literacy rates are at opposite ends of the spectrum, demonstrates this clearly. In Kerala, the overall literacy rate is reportedly 90 percent with 86 percent female literacy. By contrast, in Rajasthan, female literacy is a mere 20 percent and only 12 percent of the females are literate in rural areas.

Kerala has a matrilineal tradition in which women have a much larger measure of autonomy and freedom of movement. Kerala's women also tend to marry at a much later age compared to women in other states. Most women in Rajasthan live far more restricted lives in aggressively patriarchal communities, many of whom still practice purdah very early or even child marriages. However, all these cultural and educational advantages women have in Kerala have not translated into higher political participation. The percentage of women in the Kerala legislative assembly rose from less than one percent in 1967 to six percent in 1991. In Rajasthan, the representation of women was four percent in 1967 and reached eight percent in 1985-90. Since then it has been going down. Similarly, the state of Manipur, which has a tradition of women playing a dominant role in family and community, again due to a matrilineal heritage, never elected a single woman legislator up to 1990 - when it elected its first. A similar low level of women's representation is true for Nagaland and other North-eastern states, which are known for a less repressive culture for women. By contrast, UP, Bihar, and Madhya Pradesh, which are known for their low education levels and repressive cultural norms for women, have not only sent a relatively larger proportion of women to the Lok Sabha but have also elected relatively more women MLAs.

Post-Independence Politics In independent India, politics has proved to be very inhospitable for women. One important reason is the pervasive gender discrimination which results in making even veteran women politicians feel bypassed and ignored. For new entrants, discrimination makes it very difficult for them to establish a foothold without patronage from powerful men in the party. However, it is important to recognise that the sidelining of women in our polity goes beyond gender discrimination. It is part of a larger process in which most honest, decent people have become politically marginalised as our politics and government have become the hotbed of crooks, thugs and even outright criminals. Very few honest men or women have survived in electoral politics and kept their honesty intact.

Today the political scene has come to be dominated by anti-social elements because we have reduced our democracy to the sole ritual of the electorate casting its vote whenever called upon to do so. After they vote, the people have virtually no role in thw working of civil and other institutions. After independence, the brown sahibs, led by Nehru, who inherited power from the gora sahibs, allowed the colonial bureaucracy to strengthen its stranglehold over our civic, administrative, and political institutions from the village to the national level. Even today, a young collector in his 20s rules supreme like a colonial master over the district he governs.

He can dismiss panchayats and zilla parishads at will and people have to appear before sarkari babus as hapless supplicants for every little thing. In such an atmosphere, local leaders, including elected representatives, tend to establish a nexus with bureaucrats so that both can join in unrestrained loot and plunder of public resources. No effective monitoring mechanisms exist to restrain our netas and babus or call them to account when they systematically abuse their authority. Politics has become the quickest and shortest route to getting rich without doing any work other than brokerage. If the rules of the game remain as corrupt as they are now, only those women politicians who are good at emulating the worst of male politicians in the art of power-grabbing and plundering will be able to survive.

Career graphs of Indira Gandhi, Jayalalitha, Mayawati, Rithambara, Sheila Kaul, and a host of other prominent women in power politics is a testimony that women become as vicious, corrupt, and authoritarian as the worst of men when they occupy positions of power which demand little or no accountability. Such specimens of the female gender serve neither the cause of women nor that of society. They are as harmful for our democracy as are the Bal Thackerays, Chandraswamis, H.K.L. Bhagats and Advanis. The presence of this type of woman is neither worth fighting for nor celebrating.

This is not to suggest that I am in favour of leaving the political arena to the male crooks who dominate our Parliament and state legislatures today. Far from it. But would like to see women enter politics with a vision for restoring the health of our dysfunctional political system, to make our politics truly representative and overhaul our institutions of governance - the local corporations, police stations, courts, and various government offices in such a way that they become actually accountable to ordinary citizens in their everyday functioning.

Extra Load of Morality Many argue that to expect women to carry an extra load of morality is to make unreasonable demands of them which only strengthens the stereotype of women as self-sacrificing creatures who can be easily sidelined. I confess that I am still stuck to the perhaps somewhat outdated, naive, and romantic vision of Mahatma Gandhi regarding women entering politics not to compete with men in loot and plunder but with a view to cleanse and purify politics. While it is legitimate for women to demand a share of the pie, it is equally important to ensure the pie is worth eating and that there is enough there for everyone to share. Women's entry into politics will not change anything for the better if the overall character of politics does not improve. If women join politics in greater numbers through the present scheme of reservation this change alone is not going to create a new political culture by itself. While the inadequate representation of women in governance is a serious flaw of our democracy which needs correction, to stop at merely that would be suicidal as it will only lead to making a sizable space for women in the world of organised corruption and crime.

Politics at what cost? As things stand today, even those women who have made a mark in electoral politics find it hard to sustain their involvement unless they too become money making racketeers. For the honest, the heavy investment of time and money that is required proves too burdensome to be sustained for more than a short time. A good example from among the many accounts I have heard of the special hurdles women face in politics, is that of Sarojatai Kashikar, who was a member of the Maharashtra assembly between 1991 and 1995. Sarojatai was initially drawn into politics through her husband's close association with the Shetkari Sangathana. Before her exposure to the Sangathana, she was an ordinary housewife whose only connection with political life for years was cooking and serving her husband's colleagues in the movement. Though she was well-educated, she had no interest in or knowledge of the political world.

Table 4.3: Women's Representation in the Lok Sabha (Lower House) (Source: Election Commission of India.)

Term of Lok Sabha	Total Seats	No. of Women Members	Percentage
1952-57	489	14	2.8
1957-62	494	18	3.6
1962-67	494	30	6.0
1967-71	520	31	6.0
1971-77	520	20	3.8
1977-80	542	19	3.5
1980-84*	529	28	5.3
1984-89	542	42	7.7
1989-91[2]	523	23	4.4
1991-96[2]	536	39	7.2
1996	543	35	6.4

However, as the Sangathana leader Sharad Joshi insisted that women must participate actively in the movement, she slowly came to be one of the leading cadres of the Sangathana. In 1991, the Sangathana fielded her as a candidate for the Maharashtra state assembly elections as part of their campaign to get as many women elected as possible. Though new to electoral politics, she won by a convincing margin and within a short span of time came to be one of the most respected legislators in the state assembly.

She took her work seriously, studied the required documents, kept in good contact with her constituency and was respected even by district officials for her honesty and integrity. However, her job as an MLA required that long periods had to be spent away from home attending assembly sessions in Bombay. Since she did not feel safe living alone in the MLA's hostel in Bombay, a young brother-in-law was deputed to accompany and stay with her in Bombay. She told me that even for a middle-aged married woman like herself, to be seen chatting and freely socialising with male political colleagues was likely to be misunderstood and become cause for character assassination. To avoid this, her brother-in-law remained by her side to act as a protective shield.

In addition, in Sarojatai's case she could also count on her four other male colleagues from the Sangathana who also became MLAs at the same time as her. Having been trained in the political culture of the Sangathana, her colleagues were not only exceptionally honest and decent but also used to dealing with women as colleagues. These men acted as buffers, yet provided her the necessary communication channel with the world of politicians without her having to directly hobnob with all kinds of unsavory characters. Since they were all close and trusted friends of her husband, interaction with them provided much less scope for misunderstanding. Yet she did find herself handicapped in many respects and had to watch her every step. Hence the dependence on her young and relatively inexperienced brother-in-law.

Sarojatai's accomplishments would have been nearly impossible without her supportive husband and even more supportive sister in-law who cheerfully took over the entire load of her domestic responsibility as well as caring for her two growing sons. Fortunately, her two sons were already responsible teenagers and were cooperative, but they missed her during her long absences from home. If her kids had been small, political work would have been even more stressful.

Apart from the substantial sum of money that had to be spent on her election campaign, her husband had to spend a lot of additional money to support her politics because, unlike most other MLAs, she did not make any "extra" money. The amount of money and resources officially provided to each MLA for their salary and political work simply does not cover the actual expenses of nursing a constituency.

Due to all this, Sarojatai simply refused to stand for the recent parliamentary election though she continues to be active in Sangathana work. They say behind every great man there is usually a great woman. However, behind each politically effective woman, not just a cooperative husband is required, but an extremely supportive and resourceful extended family and in addition a strong movement-based organisation ready to encourage women into public life.

THE INHIBITING FACTORS

A key component of politics is the art of building alliances. In a culture where even formal interaction with men unconnected to one's own family is frowned upon, women are severely handicapped in politics because they cannot cultivate close association with men without jeopardising their position in the family. A woman operating on her own strength in a party filled with corrupt politicians who think nothing of slandering their own women colleagues would find the going very tough, even if she can somehow mobilise other compensatory resources by her own special efforts.

Not too long ago, Uma Bharti of the BJP was driven to a suicide attempt because of the slander campaign unleashed by her own colleagues who saw her independent mass popularity as a threat to their power. They used her supposed personal closeness to one of the BJP's respected male leaders to spread all kinds of vicious rumours about her, both within the party and in the media. The fact that politics is dominated by the most unsavoury kind of men makes most women themselves reluctant to break taboos regarding free intermixing with men. A woman risks her reputation by even being seen with many of them, whereas a man does not have to prove his credentials by such fierce avoidance. Thus women are handicapped from getting crucial information which men pick up easily from casual gossip with all kinds of people. So much of our politics is carried out in late night sessions, often over booze, where deals are made and strategies planned. Most women politicians, including the corrupt ones, don't dare to be seen participating in such sessions.

The breakdown of institutional politics in favour of gangster politics has made things much tougher for women, especially given the strict regime of restrictions that most women are made to live under. Even though most men in India favour women's political participation, this does not easily translate into relaxing restrictions on the women in their own families. Behavioral change at the family level will require consistent hard work to change cultural norms and reduce women's domestic responsibilities.

Even in educated middle class neighbourhoods of Delhi, mohalla associations are usually run by men. While a few families are willing to relax some restrictions on women and are supportive of their activism, the workload of women and the nature of their domestic responsibilities make it extremely hard for them to spare the kind of time required for making even a small difference in politics.

When I was studying the functioning of an all-women panchayat in a Maharashtra village, one of the leading members described the difficulties of keeping women active and involved, except intermittently: "For every little thing, we have to go and petition the district level officials - whether you want a road repaired or a bus service extended to your village, a water tank built or a phone connection sanctioned - each of these tasks require numerous trips to district headquarters with each trip involving loss of one full work day for a woman. Often meeting officials won't get the work done. You have to organise protests, sit on dharnas and what not.

Women simply can't spare that kind of time even if their husbands are not objecting to their participation. Men enjoy meeting officials, having chai-pani with them, because that is how they build contacts which can be encashed for personal benefit in various ways. But women are always in a hurry to get back. They don't want to hang around gossiping in tea shops, chatting with officials and *netas* - all of which seem to be a necessary part of men's political world." As long as working in the political realm involves endless petition mongering to uncaring, unaccountable authorities, as long as decision-making remains remote and in the hands of bureaucrats, as long as politics cannot be easily integrated into the everyday life of people without causing severe disturbances in domestic life, men are likely to control and dominate it.

There should be no requirement that a person become a full-time politician and make it a profession (as well as a means of livelihood) if we want meaningful participation by large numbers of women in this country's political life on a consistent, long-term basis, rather than fitful, sporadic involvement in morchas and dharnas, as happens at present. The more centralised and authoritarian a polity, the lower the involvement of women will be in it.

Additional Disadvantages By keeping more than three-quarters of India's women illiterate and providing shamelessly poor quality education to the few who manage to reach sarkari schools, the government plays a crucial role in discouraging and obstructing women's participation in public affairs. Even for participation at the panchayat level, it is no longer possible for an illiterate person to function effectively because the sarkari panchayats have been integrated into the vast bureaucratic network, with its reams of forms to fill out and its dust-covered volumes of rules and procedures.

Moreover, the rules are rendered in such opaque Hindi or regional languages that even the literate members of panchayats find it difficult to make any sense of them. Wherever the panchayat members are incapable of or diffident about handling rules and accounts, the government-appointed gram sevak simply takes control of the panchayats. Most women, especially those who are uneducated, feel helpless and lost when they are required to deal with the impenetrable maze of the bureaucratic world which defines the parameters of the panchayat's role. What appears to be a woman panchayat member's incapacity is actually proof of our system's ridiculous procedures and insensitivity to people's requirements. What goes by the name of politics in our country is an overly time consuming and debased activity. Even for those who are honest and sincere in their work, the nature of our political institutions makes it very difficult to make a real difference. Nothing comes to our citizens without sifarish and influence because the government encroaches on too many aspects of our lives in negative ways.

Our MPs and MLAs are constantly mobbed by favour-seekers and petition-mongers. They waste a good part of their time doling out favours to their supporters and people who seek their intervention in getting a water or electricity connection, a telephone or gas cylinder sanctioned, jobs or school admission, out-of-turn railway reservations from the MP quota, and generally mediating with various sarkari offices for "getting work done" (kaam karwana) since our babus don't believe in doing anything unless kicked from above or bribed from below. This includes intervening in cases of harassment by the police, corporation or other government agencies.

In addition, an MP or an MLA is expected to lobby to get funds sanctioned for repair of roads or to get sarkari approval for the opening of an engineering or medical college. Even to get a primary health centre opened or a public sector enterprise started in their constituency requires lobbying. In other words, all those things that ought to happen in the normal course of events require constant string-pulling in India.

The kind of politicians who can thrive in such an atmosphere are not likely to have the time or the skills required of a legislator such as initiating meaningful changes in government policy and making appropriate laws to translate that policy into action. This cultivation of a network of favour-seekers is essentially the only political activity commonly recognised as "political work" and "constituency building". Within this system how can a legislator do any meaningful work in her/his constituency? No matter how hard an MLA may try, she/he is not likely to succeed in getting a primary health centre or primary school of that constituency to function properly. However, very little effort is required for an MLA to become a part of the corruption network and make money by keeping the malfunctioning system intact. The constant pressure from favour-seekers means that an MP/MLA has no time for a normal family life. Women find this part of politics especially hard to cope with. That is why most of our women legislators tend to be from political families which are conditioned to withstand such a stressful life-style. No ordinary person can put up with so much strain and stay sane.

Staying Power of Women The staying power of women in politics is also limited due to the fact that while they may get support and even get to be treated as heroines if they win an election, very few women are allowed to remain politically active once they lose an election. According to Sharad Joshi, whose Shetkari Sangathana worked hard to bring large number of women into the electoral arena, it is extremely difficult to keep women politically active after they have lost an election because a woman who continues to devote time to politics even after the electoral setback gets to be looked down on as a hopeless addict, like a wayward man hooked on drugs or liquor. Therefore, unlike men, women cannot take defeat in their stride and tend to fade out soon thereafter.

Considering all this, it is perhaps not a coincidence that the few women who have developed an independent political base and are able to compete with men in electoral politics are mostly single or widowed - as for example, Uma Bharti of the BJP, Mamta Banerjee of the Congress Party, and Maneka Gandhi of the Janata Dal. These women are able to give their undivided attention to politics because there is no man to hold them back and, therefore, they are not easily cowed down by scandal or character assassination. These three women have had to wage relentless battles within their respective parties for due recognition because their popularity, mass appeal and their organisational skills which are resented by their male colleagues. Yet these women have mostly emerged triumphant because they are celebrities to their supporters.

While Indian society may not be very kind to ordinary women, it loves to celebrate women of appear and prove themsleves to be stronger than men.

In Maneka Gandhi's case, the aura around the Gandhi family name has played an important role in adding to her charisma, while both Uma Bharti and Mamta Bannerji come from very ordinary familes and were not groomed by any powerful patriarchs. Women who show extraordinary resilience, courage and the capacity to withstand character assassination get to be treated with special awe and reverence in our country. Despite all the muck-raking regarding Uma Bharti's alleged affairs, her opponents in the party have not been able to eclipse her. She is a popular cult figure among the BJP followers, far more influential in electoral campaigns of the party than even Rajmata Scindia with all her royal antecedents. However, none of these women have the clout their popularity should have earned them within their respective parties.

At the same time, it is ironic that none of these three women make a special point of mobilising other women. They would see that as a downgrading of their status if they were projected primarily as leaders of women. The more successful among women politicians do not like to be seen as representing women's interests. It is unfortunate that by and large only those who find it hard to maintain a secure foothold for themselves in elective politics tend to gravitate towards women's issues.

Politics for Ordinary Women

Our democracy will become more meaningful when ordinary women can take part in political deliberations without having to make heroic sacrifices and prove themselves stronger than men over and over again.

In the existing circumstances, even talented women cannot stay in politics on their own steam, especially if they are married and have families. Women need the following conducive conditions in order to participate effectively in the public realm:

i. A supportive family, preferably one with a political background
ii. Someone from within the extended family willing to take over a large part of the family responsibility, especially the care of her kids
iii. A good amount of surplus money in the family

Not only in India, but even in the West, very few women can count on all these factors combining together in their favour. The nuclear family and the high divorce rate in the West make it that much harder for women to give much time to sustained political activity, especially since most Western women are simultaneously engaged in employment outside the house. If a woman's day revolves around dropping off and picking up kids from creches after an eight or ten hour job outside the house, there is not much energy or time left for political work, except sporadic participation in campaigns and demonstrations. If the nature and demands of politics are such that a woman has to choose between her children and politics, most women are likely to avoid politics.

Therefore, it is crucially important for women to have more leisure for them to want to participate in politics. They tend to prefer political work that doesn't take them too far away from home on a regular basis. Thus women can be effective only in decentralised polities where decisions affecting people's lives can be taken locally.

Where Women Succeeded If we look around the world, we find that women have secured a strong political foothold only in those societies where institutions function according to well-defined democratic norms, where the crime, violence, and overall corruption levels are low, where decision-making is not concentrated in the hands of a few, and where citizens actively participate in local governance without needing to become full-time politicians. It is no coincidence that the representation of women is highest in the parliaments of the Scandinavian countries.

By contrast, in the more macho and aggressive political climate of the USA, women's representation in the Senate is barely nine percent. This is despite the long history of the militant women's movement in the United States. Apart from the above mentioned factors, family life in the Scandinavian countries has changed dramatically due to changes from above and below, allowing women relatively greater leisure and freedom. According to 1994 statistics, 66 percent of Swedish women in the age group 25-29 were never married or remained single. In the 40-49 age groups this figure drops to 16 percent - still high by Indian standards, where marriage is nearly universal. This doesn't count the people who are divorced and separated, but only those who remain single.

In Sweden, according to 1994 data, the average number of children a woman has in her entire lifetime is 1.9, and according to 1992-93 figures, 28 percent of Swedish couples were cohabiting without children. In 1990-91, Swedish women spent an average of 17 hours per week on household work excluding childcare, with men contributing six hours. In 1990-91, women had 33 hours per week for leisure activities with men having only a slight advantage with 35 hours of leisure per week.

The state provides high-quality childcare through municipal institutions and in 1993, 58 percent of kids aged one to six attended state-supported daycare centres. The state also provides "cash benefits" up to 450 days after a baby is born for both fathers and mothers of young children. There are many other special benefits provided for children who have special needs. The functional and streamlined democracies typical of Scandinavia have opened up a substantial amount of time for both women and men who are interested in political work or any other work outside the domestic sphere.

However, the support system that is enjoyed by people living in Scandinavian countries is only possible because these countries have:

- Very high income levels
- Not a very dramatic gap between the rich and the poor.
- Small and culturally homo-geneous populations
- Well-developed traditions of the state playing a social welfare role
- A substantial number of women living indepen-dently.
- Very high education levels for both men and women and high participation of women in the income earning labour force. For instance, in 1994, only five percent of women were unemployed in Sweden while the figure for unemployed men was a little higher at seven percent.
- A situation in which families are spending less and less time on housework and care of children. Interaction with "other family members", such as elderly parents, let alone other relatives, is at a minimum.

It is no wonder that having freed themselves from the domestic sphere, Scandinavian women lead the women of the world in political participation. However, this has been achieved at the very heavy cost which most of us in India may not be willing to pay. Care of others outside the family takes up about 30 minutes a week for both women and men in Sweden. By contrast, Swedish women spend 32.6 and men spend 35.2 hours a week on leisure activities.

All of this paints a picture of an increasing atomisation of human life and rapid erosion of family ties. If one compares the time involvement of Swedish parents with their children or relatives to the amount of importance given to family life in India, including time with children, old parents, relatives, neighbours, and friends, it becomes obvious why most people in India, not just women, are averse to sustained political work. However, the gains Scandinavian women have made in the public realm are indeed substantial.

In this respect, Japan provides an interesting contrast where politics at the top is highly male-dominated but at the bottom is becoming rather woman-centric. In Japan, a majority of women do not work outside the house, while men are expected to work extremely hard to support their families. Employers control not only men's long working hours, but also their leisure time when they are expected to socialise with male colleagues going in groups to bars or geisha houses. Consequently, men have hardly any time for family life. They come home too late, too tired, and leave too early to be able to take an active interest in family or neighbourhood affairs. Consequently, the whole domestic terrain and neighbourhood is left to women who have lots of free time on their hands once their husbands and kids leave the house. In addition, men are expected to hand over their earnings to women - family finances are controlled and managed mostly by women.

The male-centric traditional culture of Japan does expect women to remain servile to men and nurture them obediently. But since men are home so little, the time women spend serving and pleasing men is very small. During such time they tend to wear a Kabuki-mask-like expression and do the required rituals, only to shed that mask of servility as soon as men leave home.

Unlike women in India, they socialise with other women freely, especially in their neighbourhoods and they do not live under a regime of restrictions over their movements and interactions with the outside world, provided they are not spending too much time with other men or having extramarital affairs. Consequently, women as a group have the time and the resources to take an active interest in local neighbourhood affairs - including civic matters. The politics at this level is heavily female-centred. The famous socialist party woman leader, Takako Doi, came into prominence by quietly building a vast political base by mobilising such female networks and energy into the political mainstream.

Thus, women in Japan have carved out a special space for themselves in politics at the base level without the confrontational militancy of the Western feminists. In this case, the fact that most Japanese women are relatively leisured housewives proved to be a positive asset. It would have been much harder had they been running from high-pressured jobs, to household shopping, to creches, and to the kitchens, as most

Western women do.

All this only goes to underscore the fact that the problem is far more complex than simply that Indian women are lagging behind due to discrimination. We have to make politics worthy of women, tune it sensitively to their requirements or else even with reserved seats, only those who become like saree-wearing men will be able to survive in politics.

PAYING HOMAGE TO WOMEN IN POLITICS WHO SHAPED OUR LIVES

1. Phumzile Mlambo-Nguka

A former teacher who holds a degree in social science and an MA in philosophy, Mlambo-Nguka is a senior member of the ANC and was the director of World University Services, as well as being involved in the funding of local development organisations by Swedish and Swiss government agencies. Previously the Minister of Minerals and Energy, Mlambo-Ngcuka became South Africa's first female deputy president in June 2005, taking over the role from Jacob Zuma.

2. Condoleezza "Condi" Rice

"Condi" Rice is the first woman of colour to become the US Secretary of State; prior to this appointment (in 2005), she was the National Security Advisor. Rice has actively participated in the Bush administration's controversial "war against terrorism", placing her in the international spotlight. She also served on the administration of George Bush Senior. Forbes magazine has voted her the most powerful woman in the world.

3. Ellen Johson-Sirleaf

As Liberian president, Ellen is the first female head of state on the African continent. Despite her diminutive, grandmotherly figure, she's widely known as Liberia's "iron lady" due to her resolve and outspokenness. A Harvard- educated economist, she's been active in politics for 30 years including working as Finance Minister in the 1970s and as Africa director at the United Nations Development Programme.

4. Lindiwe Mabuza

Mabuza succeeded Cheryl Carolus as SA's High Commissioner to the UK in 2001. No newcomer to the diplomatic corps, she was active in the liberation struggle as an ANC representative in several countries before becoming the first black Ambassador to Germany in 1996. She was then made High Commissioner to Malaysia and Brunei, and served as Ambassador to the Philippines from 1999-2001. She is also a noted poet and author, and the recipient of several honorary degrees.

5. Brigalia Bam

Dr Brigalia Bam is the chairperson of the Independent Electoral Commission, chancellor of the University of Port Elizabeth, vice-chairperson of the University of South Africa and founder and president of the Women's Development Foundation. She is a qualified social worker and holds a post-graduate degree from the University of Chicago. She was formerly general secretary of the SA Council of Churches and, in 1980, worked for the Women's Programme of the International Training Food and Allied Workers' Association in Geneva. She is also noted for her active role in the struggle against sexism and racism in South Africa.

6. Luisa Diogo

In 2004 Luisa Diogo became Mozambique's first female prime minister, representing the Frelimo party; before this she occupied the post of Minister of Planning and Finance (a role she continues to hold). A mother of three, she holds several degrees in economics and worked for the World Bank as programme officer in Mozambique. She currently also heads her country's negotiations with the International Monetary Fund.

7. Joyce Piliso-Seroko

In 1999 Joyce was appointed by former President Nelson Mandela to head the first South African Commission on Engder Equality. At the end of her first term in 2002, she was re-appointed for a further five-year terms due to her outstanding skill and understanding of the complex issues involved. She is also a member of the Eskom Council and a committee member of the Women's Development foundation, among other notable positions.

8. Patricia De Lille

Known for her outspokenness and fearless criticism of corruption, Patricia is the first black South African woman to lead a political party (The Independent Democrats) which she formed in 2003 after breaking away from the Pan-African Congress. A former anti-apartheid activist and trade unionist, she was the first woman to be elected to the executive of the National Council of Trade Unions (NACTU), for which she served as national vice-president.

9. Nkosazana Dlamini-Zuma

South Africa's Minister of Foreign Affairs, Dlamini-Zuma was a former political activist and an active member of the ANCE before going into exile. In 1994 she was appointed as the country's Minister of Health and stirred up controversy after legalising abortion. She was also noted for enacting the Tobacco Products Control Bill, which has made it illegal for anyone to smoke in public places. She is the former wife of Jacob Zuma.

10. Aung San Suu Kyi

The "Mandela of the East", Aung San Suu Kyi is an activist who has spent nearly 13 of the past 18 years either in prison or under house arrest, detained by the military government ruling her homeland, Burma. A Nobel Peace prize winner, Suu Kyi has devoted her life to bringing about democratic rule in her country.

Her commitment to her cause has been at great personal cost: she does not get to see her two sons (who live outside of Burma); and, in 1999, her husband succumbed to terminal cancer - without being granted permission to enter Burma and see his wife on last time before he died. Suu Kyie is currently under house arrest, and little has been seen of her since 1999.

VIOLENCE AGAINST WOMEN LIMITS THEIR POLITICAL AIM

Violence is one of the major influencing factors to obstruct womens' participation in governance. Women are making steady inroads into almost every profession in South Asia these days. Yet, when it comes to politics, why are many women politicians not seen? The reason, according to a non governmental oganisation (NGO), is violence-more psychological than physical -against women in politics.

Representatives of the South Asia Partnership (SAP), an international organisation that promotes democracy through the civil society came together on Monday to discuss the various aspects of this disturbing fact that has, until now, not been highlighted, reports IANS.

"Women participating in politics are victimised by both direct and invisible violence, which is one of the major influencing factors to obstruct their participation in governance," Savitri Goonsekre of Sri Lanka said.

Character assassination, kidnapping of their children, rape and even murder of winner women politicians by opposition party members after losing elections, social boycott for being involved in politics, breakage of relationships, ill treatment by husbands...there are a whole lot of reasons which discourage women from entering the field, she said.

"Despite the fact that most countries have signed the Convention on the Elimination of All Forms of Discrimination against Women (CEDAW), a country like mine (Sri Lanka) has just five per cent women in the National Assembly, which is shameful," Goonsekre added.

Chandni Joshi of Nepal said that although it will be very difficult to look for any data on violence against women in politics, it exists everywhere.

"There are one million women involved in the panchayati raj in India, yet they continue to be faceless, not being able to do much for their own upliftment. The patriarchal society ensures that the reins of the panchayat, even if the woman is the sarpanch (village head), lie with the husband," Joshi, who has worked in India for 14 years, said.

"In the Indian panchayat set up, the discrimination is very subtle. A women sarpanch sits on the floor, while her male counterpart will sit on a chair,"Martha Farrell of India said.

Women are not allowed to speak in the panchayat meeting and any kind of question from them is discouraged. Overall, in both rural and urban set-up during elections, harassment of women is considered as nothing extraordinary, she said.

One of the major drawbacks which women face in politics, according to Farrell, is that the Supreme Court guideline against sexual harassment of women in work places does not consider women politicians.

"Just 1.3 per cent of India's budgetary allocation is for women's development and empowerment while many other South Asian countries allocate 3.5 per cent. Policies for development of women exist, but are not implemented. These are all bottlenecks," Joshi added.

There is some good news too. Afghanistan's constitution guarantees non-discrimination and equality of women and men and reserves a 25 per cent share of seats for women parliamentarians in the National Assembly.

In Bangladesh in the general elections, for the first time the number of women voters exceeded the male voters. In Nepal, there is a 33 per cent representation for women in parliament.

"A lot more has to be done to encourage women to come into politics for the sake of allround development of our country. Women's issues should not just be another publicity gimmick pointer in political parties' manifestos," Farrell said.

REDEFINING THE POLITICS OF PRESENCE

What is the value of women's representation in Panchayati Raj Institutions (PRIs), for themselves, for the political process, and for development in India? Nearly two years ago, intrigued by the 73rd Amendment and its mandated reservation of 1/3 of all seats for women, I set out to try to qualitatively answer this question. Over the course of a year (1997-98), I analyzed several political, sociological, and feminist theories and case studies on political presence and empowerment, met with a number of government officials, academics, and activists, and interviewed panches and community members in four villages, two in Rajasthan and two in Kerala. What follows is a summary of my findings and ideas.

Why should reservations exist at all?

Various theorists have argued that reservations are desirable for at least six reasons: (1) Elected women will served as role models to other young and old women, encouraging them to participate in politics and even contest future elections. (2) It is a matter of justice that women be included in political structures, as they constitute 50% of the population and should not be absent from spheres of power. (3) Elected women will bring "women's interests" to the formal political sphere. Because men do not understand "women's interests", male-dominated political institutions either leave them off of the agenda, or they act in a manner that indirectly or directly damages women's position. (4) Elected women will transform the very culture of politics. This argument relies on an assumption that women are more caring, cooperative individuals.

Therefore, less prone to factionalism and corruption, women will be able to transform today's 'dirty politics' into a more equitable, kinder, and participatory politics. (5) Although most representatives are confined to vote along the lines of their political parties, they have a few moments of autonomy. In these opportunities for independent thinking, the character and identity of the politician is significant. Women - through their various identities - can therefore contribute to the political discourse by adding their unique perspectives. (6) There is a symbolic relevance to women's reservations. The quotas dismantle the status quo and let women feel, and be seen as, represented in the formal decision-making process.

Yet, while many theorists have speculated on the need for and impact of reservations for women, few had been able to practically understand reservations in a real-world environment. However, this is not their fault. Throughout the world's representative democracies, despite the fact that across the board few women are present in formal political institutions, quotas for political representation are rare, if not non-existent. India's decision to include reservations for women, Scheduled Tribes, and Scheduled Castes in the Panchayati Raj Institutions is therefore groundbreaking and unique. The closest parallel is in Sweden and Norway, who implemented a 40% quota for women's representation in political parties.

RESERVATIONS IN INDIA

Not only are reservations unusual in the world context, it is also surprising that they appeared in India at all. Judging from accounts of the passage of the legislation, it appears that the political elite installed quotas in the absence of an organized movement devoted to this goal. Reservations in India did not emerge out of a typical historical pattern (of industrialization, urbanization, the entrance of women into the formal wage-earning sector, and their subsequent demands for political representation), nor did the Indian women's movement push the formal political sector for the quotas. Indeed, the women's movement in the early 1990's was primarily mobilizing around issues of dowry, rape/sexual harassment, and prohibition.

Using direct action techniques and other informal strategies, women tended to push civil and political institutions to uphold their own laws. They were not challenging the gender ratios of those institutions, and they were certainly not demanding formalized entry into those institutions. Finally, the fact that the reservations would apply to Panchayati Raj Institutions makes their appearance even more striking. In the vast majority of rural areas, women rarely exercise power in the formal political sphere, but rather express their authority and power in the more informal spaces of the home, the commons, and community associations.

In fact, women appear to prefer informal political spaces over formal institutions. As Amrita Basu highlights in Two Faces of Protest, adivasi women in Maharashtra were able to better exercise their political power in direct action organizations. Free from having to tailor their language or action to mainstream politics, the women were able to mobilize quickly and use spontaneous tactics (even songs!) to carry out their political agendas. She contrasts the freedom of informal politics with the constraints of formal politics, by giving the example of women belonging to the Communist Party of India (Marxist) in West Bengal. There, women felt stifled by the political organization and structures, which tended to reinforce or reshape dominant social patterns, thereby relegating women to lesser work and fewer leadership opportunities. They did not offer women the space for spontaneous action, for unusual tactics, or for placing their agenda on the table. Basu's work helps explain why perhaps the thrust for women's reservations did not come from women themselves.

So, where did the impetus for reservations for women come from? Some have argued that the political parties, who approved the 73rd amendment in record time, were motivated by noble intentions; they wanted to "strengthen the position of the poor and weaker sections in rural India." However, I suspect that the majority of (if not all) political parties supported quotas for women, because they did not expect women's participation to be empowering. Instead, perhaps they assumed that women would take on a passive, subdued role in the formal political sector. This weak presence would enable parties to easily dominate the representative and forward their own agendas through them.

There is certainly historical and contemporary evidence to support this speculation. In two very different contexts (the nationalist movement of pre-Independent India and Japan of the late 1970's), Partha Chatterjee and Susan Pharr describe how women's roles in formal political spheres took on a subordinate, 'traditional' character. As Chatterjee describes, during the nationalist struggle, "woman" was essentially equated with "nation" and represented the values of "self-sacrifice, benevolence, and devotion." Central to this ideas were the contrasts between the material and spiritual, Western and Indian, modern and traditional, and men and women.

Because women were representative of the true India - of its spiritual, traditional world - they were invited to participate in the Independence movement, but only as long as their involvement did not threaten the prevailing notions of femininity. Women could not break from their ascribed feminine roles, nor empower themselves through the movement, for to do so would be to contest the value of the Indian nation as a whole. Similarly, in Japan, Pharr depicts another example of "presence without empowerment" in her study of Japanese women politicians. She labels them "neo-traditional activists," as their entry into politics, their understanding of their political role, and their political causes/ ideologies all depend upon a male figure (typically a father, brother, or husband). While neither Pharr nor Chatterjee are speaking about women in the context of PRIs, their insights into "presence without empowerment" help explain what may have motivated those who supported the emergence of reservations in India. Now, the question becomes, given this history and contextual background, what can be the impact of women in formal political institutions?

Notion of representation

Descriptive representation refers to the physical fact of particular individuals being located in political, economic, social institutions. It is the symbolic effect of quotas for women's representation; it simply means that they are physically in these institutions and everyone can see them there. Substantive representation refers to the substantial content of one's representation. In other words, it is the influence or impact of one's presence on the political discourse, the culture of politics, the political party, or political outcomes. It is the substantial content of one's presence. Personally transformative representation deals with the impact of one's representation on oneself, one's identity, one's meaning-making systems, and one's world. While the other two forms of representation are essentially external, this aspect of representation deals with the internal and the individual herself. It is neglected by most theorists and academics and rarely enters the vocabulary of political science.

These three forms of representation can be extended into a language of interests. Drawing upon the work of Anna Jonasdottir, the concept of interests into two connected aspects: form and content. The form aspect refers to the demand for participation in society's public affairs and spaces; the content aspect deals with the substantive values emerging from political activity. To these two aspects, I add the personally transformative interest. That is, alongside interests in shaping political content or holding political presence, women also have an interest in using the political process to transform them, develop their capacities, and alter their roles.

Broadening the definition of interests, in this way, allows us to go beyond the narrowly understood concept of "women's interests," which tends to confine women to issues of reproduction, marriage, and sexuality. Although these three issues have validity and relevance to nearly all Indian women, such a limited sense of interests is problematic for at least three reasons. First, it constructs women as generic beings and reduces them to biological traits, thereby denying the important roles that cultural context, caste, religion, socioeconomic status, and education play in determining interests. These narrow understandings deny the diversity and complexity of women. Second, by limiting women to issues reproduction, marriage, and sexuality, women are viewed as unable to put other "non-gendered" issues on the political agenda, such as employment, land, housing, and water. Nor are women offered space to articulate their larger visions of development, the system, or change. Thirdly, by calling these women's interests, we deepen the already large chasm between men and women. We fail to see the role that men play in these areas and therefore prevent constructive action by men (i.e., how can they help to solve or prevent this problem?). Instead of thinking of our interests and aspirations as human beings, and of how we all have a responsibility to think and act in ways that nurture and benefit all of us, we close the door to dialogue, common interests, and generative action.

This discussion brings me to the particular context of Panchayati Raj Institutions. What do these three notions of representation and of interests mean for rural Indian women in an environment of decentralized democracy? To get a sense of how these ideas play out in an empirical context, we must turn to the structural and substantive limits of women's representation in Panchayati Raj Institutions.

OBSTACLES TO WOMEN'S EFFECTIVE PARTICIPATION

To understand the obstacles to women's participation, we must first comprehend the historical debate surrounding PRIs. Taking a break from academic parlance and would like to imagine a conversation between Mohandas K. Gandhi, B.R. Ambedkar, and Jawaharlal Nehru to illustrate the various sides of the Panchayati Raj controversy. The issues they discuss have relevance for us still today, as we struggle to make sense of our roles, not only as political actors, but as change agents in an increasingly complex world.

Gandhi: Part of the goal of the Freedom Struggle was the achievement of village swaraj. How can achieve this with a tight, centralized government, where British elite rule is simply replaced by Indian elite rule? In a country as large and diverse as India, who lives in her 700,000 villages, the masses would be excluded and untouched.

Ambedkar: Why should the village become the locus of the political structure? The village is a 'cesspool, a den of ignorance, narrow-mindedness, and communalism.' Why would we want to entrust political rule and development to it? Scheduled Castes and Scheduled Tribes will be oppressed by the upper caste ruling elite. In fact, upper castes will have total control in an unregulated decentralized system.

Nehru: Perhaps we can attempt some type of modified centralization. We can institute Panchayati Raj, cooperatives, and other village-level organizations. But instead of permitting limitless authority by upper castes, we can monitor and regulate the panchayats at the state level. That is, the center and the states will limit the autonomy of the panchayat by controlling its finances, planning, projects, and administration. It will be a face of decentralization with a heart of centralization.

Gandhi: What is the point of such a deception? If the state and the center will maintain power and continue to exclude the people from participation, then why bother? If PRIs had financial, administrative, and conceptual autonomy, then we would not need to fear Ambedkar's fears. Panchayats could enhance the social and economic development of India and make swaraj a reality.

Narsimha Rao (in a time machine): But because we realistically fear village ignorance and hatred, and because we (the state and the center) have a difficult time giving up control. The 73rd amendment to the Indian Constitution will strengthen Panchayati Raj Institutions, ensure them with certain developmental responsibilities, and guarantee representation from the marginalized segments of society. But the federal and state governments will still have much of the financial and conceptual control. The state will devolve some responsibility to the panchayats, but it will not relinquish total power.

This conversation not only highlights the many competing visions of PRIs, it also illustrates the subsequent history of Panchayati Raj in India. Though originally implemented with Nehru's vision of modified centralization, PRIs quickly deteriorated in the decades following Independence into Ambedkar's strong version of centralization. In 1993, PRIs were reintroduced as modified decentralization by former Prime Minister Narsimha Rao.

Though lingering in the background Gandhiji's vision of PRIs remains unrealized. He saw the village panchayat as "an oceanic circle whose center will be the individual always ready to perish for the village, the latter ready to perish for the circle of villages, till at last the whole becomes one life composed of individuals, never aggressive in their arrogance, but ever humble, sharing the majesty of the economic circle of which they are integral units."

In other words, in spite of hierarchies related to caste, tribe, gender, education, etc., Gandhiji believed that Panchayati Raj would offer opportunities for real participation at the rural level, in which the individual saw herself as part of the greater whole. Therefore, she would engage with others to improve herself as well as the community at large. In Gandhiji's decentralized democracy, development would grow out of the village, where people would collectively work to conceptualize what they meant by 'development' and 'progress' and then learn and act together in ways that allowed them to realize their visions and common aspirations.

Unfortunately far from Gandhiji's vision, what we have today in Panchayati Raj Institutions are a series of structural constraints and contextual conditions that have failed to empower women, their panchayats, or village communities as a whole. Through a critical examination of the State Panchayati Raj Acts of Kerala and Rajasthan in my longer thesis, I reveal how PRIs are structurally disempowered. While I will not expand upon the details here, in brief, the overarching impediment to the effective functioning of PRIs is the tension in the relationship between state and local bodies.

As currently structured in both Rajasthan and Kerala, the panchayats have a hollow authority, for they lack executive power. State-appointed civil servants are used to implement predetermined schemes, keep control of panchayat minutes, and control panchayat budgets in all three tiers of the PRI system. If the state government carries such influence in the functioning and decision-making processes of the panchayat, where is the space for creativity, autonomy, and leadership in the panchayat? For example, schemes run out of the state and center, like Indira Avas Yojana, Jivan Dara, and Integrated Rural Development Program, are particularly stifling. They decide the needs and plans of the panchayat in advance, and thus determine the path of development all villages are to follow. Yet, in preventing active conceptualization, planning, implementation, and evaluation by the panchayats themselves, such schemes fail to recognize diversity and knowledge and instead reinforce a financial and conceptual dependence on the state.

The State Panchayati Raj Acts illustrate further structural limitations. The overlap in responsibilities between the various levels (district, block, and village) of Panchayati Raj, the lack of connection and dialogue between the levels, the division of functions in mandatory functions and discretionary functions (Kerala) and the absence of technical sharing among the levels (Rajasthan) all damage the panchayat's ability to participate in the process of decentralized democratic development.

If we pay particular attention to representation by women, the Acts reveal additional structural impediments. For example, the Rajasthan Panchayat Act requires that the sarpanch be able to read and write Hindi. Although this clause appears to be gender-neutral, given Rajasthan's low rate of literacy among rural women, it is not for three reasons: It limits the number of possible women candidates, it may exclude the best candidates, and it places an inordinate (and in my view, undue) emphasis on literacy. Similarly, the mechanisms of election (direct vs. indirect), the quorum process, and the electoral rotation process are all impediments to women's substantive and personally transformative representation.

The sociocultural context is therefore also critical to understanding the obstacles to women's representation in PRIs. Again, while this is expanded upon in my full paper, here, I will only highlight two contextual factors – the negative stereotypes of women in rural Rajasthan and the hierarchical political party system in Kerala - that affect women's representation. In the two panchayats I studied in Rajasthan, the stereotypes of women focused on their incompetence, their lack of merit, and were highly correlated with their levels of literacy. As one up-sarpanch explained, "Because they are illiterate, women do not know how to think. If they thought, they would speak." Nearly quoting Susan Pharr, another panch explained that women only stood for election, because they were pushed by their male relatives. Therefore, they could not be judged by their own personal merit like male candidates were. Confronted with such attitudes, it is not surprising that low self-esteem and lack of confidence appear to be a problem for women panches in rural Rajasthan.

On the other hand, in Kerala, it appeared that the party structure stifled women's political participation. While the CPI(M), the party in power during my research, seems to acknowledge that women have a place in the decision-making process, it confines that place to the number of reserved seats - no more, no less. Leadership by women does not appear to overstep unwritten sociopolitical boundaries, as the party maintains its own established hierarchies. For example, although women were present in the Gram Sabha I visited, and they participated in the village committees organized under Kerala's People's Planning Campaign, they did not take on leadership roles, nor were they extremely vocal participants.

Despite these bleak pictures, there are a few bright spots. For example, women in one of the Rajasthani panchayats expressed that they had gained a knowledge of public affairs and they realized that they too could do public work. In Kerala, the majority of attendees in the Gram Sabha I visited were women, who saw themselves as community role models. Although these examples may seem small in the face of larger problems, they do offer us foundations upon which to suggest recommendations for change.

Way Forward

Though the experiences of Keralite and Rajasthani women differ in content and magnitude, women in both states must still face structural impediments from their Panchayati Raj Acts and sociocultural constraints in their environments. In this way, they both share the dilemma of presence without empowerment. How do we move forward and facilitate true representation - descriptive, substantive, and personally transformative - for all women?

In my original paper, I had two major recommendations. The first was to reconstruct the role of the Gram Sabha; the second was to alter the positions of governmental and non-governmental organizations in the process of decentralization. With regards to the Gram Sabha, I recommended that the power to monitor the panchayat be transferred from the state to the community.

This redirected accountability would give an outlet to women panches for redressing grievances against the panchayat, such as corruption and abuses of the quorum process. It would also ensure a check on the financial expenditures and projects of the panchayat. Finally, it would give the entire community a chance to express its vision of and interests in development. It would open the conceptual door and shift the development dialogue from top-down to bottom-up.

I also proposed that governmental and non-governmental organizations rethink their roles. Instead of continuing in their current roles of taking power and control over the development process from the local people, they could cooperate with PRIs, offering technical assistance, support services, and civic training to panches and to the Gram Sabha, as requested. The state could further reduce its overall involvement, by eliminating its schemes and administration over the panchayat.

However, I realize that much has happened since I conducted my study in 1997. Another panchayat election is upon us, the center has introduced legislative acts that have given more power to the Gram Sabhas and to tribal areas, and a number of governmental and non-governmental organizations have implemented training programs for panches. I am also more aware of the tremendous strain (and drain) upon villages today. Globalization, liberalization, national debt, a ubiquitous mass media, increasing consumerism, urbanization, growing violence, loss of land and water, frustrated and cynical youth, dehumanizing schools and health facilities, the disappearance of languages, cultures, and knowledge systems - the list of challenges faced by the villages (and cities as well) seems endless. And I realize that simple 'representation' - whether by women or anyone - in a state-driven decentralized governance system will not be enough to mitigate these problems or to create new realities.

The time has come for more meaningful action by all us. Villagers and city-dwellers, governmental and non-governmental organizations, must begin to rethink their visions of 'development' and 'progress' and engage in serious learning, unlearning, and relearning processes. People, of all castes, tribes, socioeconomic backgrounds, ages, and genders will have to work together to redefine their notions of identity and their relationships to one another in order to build these collective visions and undertake radical efforts for change. I think it is time to move from a culture of representation to a culture of learning. Each of us must begin to take responsibility for ourselves, for the collective, and for our common humanity if we are to survive - much less live and grow - into the next century.

5

Eminent Women Politicians

INDIRA GANDHI

Indira Priyadarshini Gandhi (19 November 1917 – 31 October 1984) was the Prime Minister of the Republic of India for three consecutive terms from 1966 to 1977 and for a fourth term from 1980 until her assassination in 1984, a total of fifteen years. She was India's first and, to date, only female Prime Minister.

Born in the politically influential Nehru Family, she grew up in an intensely political atmosphere. Despite the same last name, she is of no relation to the statesman Mohandas Gandhi. Her grandfather, Motilal Nehru, was a prominent Indian nationalist leader. Her father, Jawaharlal Nehru, was a pivotal figure in the Indian independence movement and the first Prime Minister of Independent India. Returning to India from Oxford in 1941, she became involved in the Indian Independence movement.

In the 1950s, she served her father unofficially as a personal assistant during his tenure as the first Prime Minister of India. After her father's death in 1964, she was appointed as a member of the Rajya Sabha by the President of India and became a member of Lal Bahadur Shastri's cabinet as Minister of Information and Broadcasting.

The then Congress Party President K. Kamaraj was instrumental in making Indira Gandhi the Prime Minister after the sudden demise of Shastri. Gandhi soon showed an ability to win elections and outmaneuver opponents through populism. She introduced more left-wing economic policies and promoted agricultural productivity. A decisive victory in the 1971 war with Pakistan was followed by a period of instability that led her to impose a state of emergency in 1975; she paid for the authoritarian excesses of the period with three years in opposition. Returned to office in 1980, she became increasingly involved in an escalating conflict with separatists in Punjab that eventually led to her assassination by her own bodyguards in 1984.

EARLY LIFE

Indira Nehru Gandhi was born on 19 November 1917 to Pandit Jawaharlal Nehru and his young wife, Kamala Nehru. She was their only child. The Nehru family can trace their ancestry to the Brahmins of Jammu and Kashmir and Delhi. Motilal Nehru, grandfather of Indira Nehru was a wealthy lawyer of Allahabad in Uttar Pradesh. Motilal Nehru was one of the most prominent members of the Indian National Congress in pre-Gandhi times and would go on to author the Nehru Report, the people's choice for a future Indian system of government as opposed to the British system. Her father Jawaharlal Nehru was a well-educated barrister and was a popular leader of the Indian Independence Movement. At the time of Indira's birth, Nehru entered the independence movement under the leadership of Mahatma Gandhi.

Growing up in the sole care of her mother, who was sick and alienated from the Nehru household, Indira developed strong protective instincts and a loner personality. Her grandfather and father continually being enmeshed in national politics also made mixing with her peers difficult. She had conflicts with her father's sisters, including Vijayalakshmi Pandit, and these continued into the political world.

In her father's autobiography, Toward Freedom, he writes that the police frequently came to the family home while he was in prison and took away pieces of furniture as payment toward the fines the Government imposed on him. He says,

"Indira, my four-year-old daughter, was greatly annoyed at this continuous process of despoliation and protested to the police and expressed her strong displeasure. I am afraid those early impressions are likely to color her future views about the police force generally."

Indira created the Vanara Sena movement for young girls and boys which played a small but notable role in the Indian Independence Movement, conducting protests and flag marches, as well as helping Congress politicians circulate sensitive publications and banned materials. In an often-told story, she smuggled out from her father's police-watched house an important document in her schoolbag that outlined plans for a major revolutionary initiative in the early 1930s.

STUDYING IN EUROPE

In 1936, her mother, Kamala Nehru, finally succumbed to tuberculosis after a long struggle. Indira was 18 at the time and thus never experienced a stable family life during her childhood. While studying at Somerville College, University of Oxford, England, during the late 1930s, she became a member of the radical pro-independence London based India League.

In early 1940, Indira spent time in a rest home in Switzerland to recover from chronic lung disease. As she had during her childhood, she maintained her long-distance relationship with her father in the form of long letters. They argued about politics.

In her years in continental Europe and the UK, she met a young Parsi man active in politics, Feroze Gandhi (no relation to Mohandas Gandhi). After returning to India, Feroze Gandhi grew close to the Nehru family, especially to Indira's mother Kamala Nehru and Indira herself. Feroze helped nurse the ailing Kamala too.

MARRIAGE TO FEROZE GANDHI

When Indira and Feroze Gandhi returned to India, they were in love and had decided to get married, despite doctors' advice.

Indira liked Feroze's openness, sense of humour and self-confidence. Nehru did not like the idea of his daughter marrying so early and sought Mahatma Gandhi's help to dissuade their love relationship. The lady in love was adamant and the marriage took place in March 1942 according to Hindu rituals.

Feroze and Indira were both members of the Indian National Congress, and when they took part in the Quit India Movement in 1942, they were both arrested. After independence, Feroze went on to run for election and became a member of parliament from Uttar Pradesh.

After the birth of their two sons, Rajiv Gandhi and Sanjay Gandhi, the couple lead a separated life due to some conflict, until 1958. Shortly after his re-election, Feroze suffered a heart attack, which dramatically healed their broken marriage. But the love did not last for many years as Feroze died in September 1960.

The Nehru family - Motilal Nehru is seated in the center, and standing (L to R) are Jawaharlal Nehru, Vijayalakshmi Pandit, Krishna Hutheesing, Indira, and Ranjit Pandit; Seated: Swaroop Rani, Motilal Nehru and Kamala Nehru (circa 1927).

EARLY LEADERSHIP

President of the Indian National Congress. During 1959 and 1960, Gandhi ran for and was elected the President of the Indian National Congress. Her term of office was uneventful. She also acted as her father's chief of staff. Nehru was known as a vocal opponent of nepotism, and she did not contest a seat in the 1962 elections.

MINISTER OF INFORMATION AND BROADCASTING

Nehru died on 27 May 1964, and Indira, at the urgings of the new Prime Minister Lal Bahadur Shastri, contested elections and joined the Government, being immediately appointed Minister for Information and Broadcasting. She went to Madras when the riots over Hindi becoming the national language in non-Hindi speaking state of Tamilnadu. There she spoke to government officials, soothed the anger of community leaders and supervised reconstruction efforts for the affected areas.

Shastri and senior Ministers were embarrassed, owing to their lack of such initiative. Minister Gandhi's actions were probably not directly aimed at Shastri or her own political elevation. She reportedly lacked interest in the day-to-day functioning of her Ministry, but was media-savvy and adept at the art of politics and image-making.

"During the succession struggles after 1965 between Mrs. Gandhi and her rivals, the central Congress [party] leadership in several states moved to displace upper caste leaders from state Congress [party] organizations and replace them with backward caste persons and to mobilize the votes of the latter castes to defeat its rivals in the state Congress [party] and in the opposition. The consequences of these interventions, some of which may justly be perceived as socially progressive, have nevertheless often had the consequences of intensifying inter-ethnic regional conflicts...

While the Indo-Pakistani War of 1965 was ongoing, Gandhi was vacationing in the border region of Srinagar. Although warned by the Army that Pakistani insurgents had penetrated very close to the city, she refused to relocate to Jammu or Delhi and instead rallied local government and welcomed the media attention.

The Pakistan attack was successfully repelled, and Prime Minister Shastri in January 1966 signed a peace agreement with Pakistan's Ayub Khan, mediated by the Soviets in Tashkent. A few hours later, Shastri was dead of a heart attack.

The Indian National Congress President K. Kamaraj was then instrumental in making Indira Gandhi as Prime Minister, despite the opposition from Morarji Desai who was later defeated by the members of the Congress Parliamentary Party, where Indira Gandhi beat Morarji Desai by 355 votes to 169 to become the fifth Prime Minister of India and the first woman to hold that position.

PRIME MINISTER (FIRST TERM)

Domestic Politics

When Mrs. Gandhi became Prime Minister in 1966 the Congress was split in two factions, the socialists led by Mrs. Gandhi, and the conservatives led by Morarji Desai. Rammanohar Lohia called her Gungi Gudiya which means 'Dumb Doll'. The internal problems showed in the 1967 election where the Congress lost nearly 60 seats winning 297 seats in the 545 seat Lok Sabha. She had to accommodate Desai as Deputy Prime Minister of India and Finance Minister of India. In 1969 after many disagreements with Desai, the Indian National Congress split. She ruled with support from Socialist and Communist Parties for the next two years. In the same year, in July 1969 she nationalized banks.

War with Pakistan in 1971

Pakistan army conducted widespread atrocities against the civilian populations of East Pakistan. An estimated 10 million refugees fled to India, causing financial hardship and instability in the country. To solve the refugee problem, Indira Gandhi declared war on Pakistan, helping the East Pakistanis gain their independence. The United States under Richard Nixon supported Pakistan, and mooted a UN resolution warning India against going to war. Nixon apparently disliked Indira personally, referring to her as a "witch" and "clever fox" in his private communication with Secretary of State Henry Kissinger (now released by the State Department). Indira signed the Treaty of Friendship and Cooperation, resulting in political support and a Soviet veto at the UN. India was victorious in the 1971 war,. and Bangladesh was born.

Foreign policy

She invited the new Pakistani President Zulfikar Ali Bhutto to Shimla for a week-long summit. After the near-failure of the talks, the two heads of state eventually signed the Shimla Agreement, which bound the two countries to resolve the Kashmir dispute by negotiations and peaceful means. Due to her antipathy for Nixon, relations with the United States grew distant, while relations with the Soviet Union grew closer.

Indira Gandhi was criticized by some for not making the Line of Control a permanent border while a few critics even believed that Pakistan-administered Kashmir should have been extracted from Pakistan, whose 93, 000 prisoners of war were under Indian control. But the agreement did remove immediate United Nations and third party interference, and greatly reduced the likelihood of Pakistan launching a major attack in the near future. By not demanding total capitulation on a sensitive issue from Bhutto, she had allowed Pakistan to stabilize and normalize. Trade relations were also normalized, though much contact remained frozen (sealed) for years.

Devaluation of the Rupee

During the late 1960s, Indira's administration decreed 40% devaluation in the value of the Indian Rupee from 4 to 7 to the US Dollar to boost trade.

Nuclear Weapons Program

A national nuclear program was started by Mrs. Gandhi in 1967, in response to the nuclear threat from the People's Republic of China and to establish India's stability and security interests as independent from those of the nuclear superpowers. In 1974, India successfully conducted an underground nuclear test, unofficially code named as "Smiling Buddha", near the desert village of Pokhran in Rajasthan. Describing the test as for peaceful purposes, India became the world's youngest nuclear power.

Green Revolution

Richard Nixon and Indira Gandhi in 1971 had a deep personal antipathy that coloured bilateral relations.

Special agricultural innovation programs and extra government support launched in the 1960s finally transformed India's chronic food shortages into surplus production of wheat, rice, cotton and milk. Rather than relying on food aid from the United States - headed by a President whom Mrs. Gandhi disliked considerably (the feeling was mutual: to Nixon, Indira was "the old witch"), the country became a food exporter. That achievement, along with the diversification of its commercial crop production, has become known as the "Green Revolution". At the same time, the White Revolution was an expansion in milk production which helped to combat malnutrition, especially amidst young children. 'Food security', as the program was called, was another source of support for Mrs. Gandhi in the years leading up to 1975.

Established in the early 1960s, the Green Revolution was the unofficial name given to the Intense Agricultural District Program (IADP) which sought to insure abundant, inexpensive grain for urban dwellers upon whose support Gandhi-as indeed all Indian politicians-heavily depended. The program was based on four premises: 1) New varieties of seed(s), 2) Acceptance of the necessity of the chemicalization of Indian agriculture, i.e. fertilizers, pesticides, weed killers, etc., 3) A commitment to national and international cooperative research to develop new and improved existing seed varieties, 4) The concept of developing a scientific, agricultural institutions in the form of land grant colleges. Lasting about ten years, the program was ultimately to bring about a tripling of wheat production, a lower but still impressive increase of rice; while there was little to no increase (depending on area, and adjusted for population growth) of such cereals as millet, gram and coarse grain, though these did, in fact, retain a relatively stable yield.

1971 ELECTION VICTORY AND SECOND TERM (1971-1975)

Indira's government faced major problems after her tremendous mandate of 1971. The internal structure of the Congress Party had withered following its numerous splits, leaving it entirely dependent on her leadership for its election fortunes. *Garibi Hatao* (Stop Poverty) was the theme for Gandhi's 1971 bid. The slogan and the proposed anti-poverty programs that came with it were designed to give Gandhi an independent national support, based on rural and urban poor. This would allow her to bypass the dominant rural castes both in and of state and local government; likewise the urban commercial class. And, for their part, the previously voiceless poor would at last gain both political worth and political weight.

The programs created through Garibi Hatao, though carried out locally, were funded, developed, supervised, and staffed by New Delhi and the Indian National Congress party. "These programs also provided the central political leadership with new and vast patronage resources to be disbursed... throughout the country. "Scholars and historians now agree as to the extent of the failure of Garibi Hatao in alleviating poverty - only about 4% of all funds allocated for economic development went to the three main anti-poverty programs, and precious few of these ever reached the 'poorest of the poor' - and the empty sloganeering of the program was mainly used instead to engender populist support for Gandhi's re-election.

Verdict of electoral malpractice

On 12 June 1975 the High Court of Allahabad declared Indira Gandhi's election to the Lok Sabha void on grounds of electoral malpractice. In an election petition filed by Raj Narain (who had repeatedly contested her Parliamentary constituency of Rae Bareli without success), he had alleged several minor instances of using government resources for campaigning. The court thus ordered her to be removed from her seat in Parliament and banned from running in elections for six years. The Prime Minister must be a member of either the Lok Sabha (lower house in the Parliament of India) or the Rajya Sabha (the upper house of the Parliament). Thus, this decision effectively removed her from office.

Protests and civil disobedience

When Indira appealed the decision and declared she would continue to serve the people "till her last breath", the opposition parties and their supporters, eager to gain political capital from the situation, rallied en masse calling for her resignation. The sheer number of strikes by unions and protesters paralyzed life in many states. To strengthen this movement, J. P. Narayan called upon the police to disobey orders if asked to fire on unarmed crowds. Public disenchantment with her government combined with hard economic times, and huge crowds of protesters surrounded the Parliament building and her residence in Delhi, demanding her resignation.

A still from Anand Patwardhan's first documentary Waves of Revolution, about the unrest in Bihar, distributed clandestinely within India and smuggled out in sections to create awareness abroad.

Indira had already been accused of authoritarianism. By using her strong parliamentary majority, her ruling Congress Party had amended the Constitution and altered the balance of power between the Centre and the States in favour of the Central Government. She had twice imposed "President's Rule" under Article 356 of the Constitution by declaring states ruled by opposition parties as "lawless and chaotic", and thus seizing control. In addition, elected officials and the administrative services resented the growing influence of Sanjay Gandhi, who had become Gandhi's close political adviser at the expense of men like P. N. Haksar, Gandhi's previous adviser during her rise to power. In response to her new tendency for authoritarian use of power, public figures and former freedom-fighters like Jaya Prakash Narayan, Satyendra Narayan Sinha and Acharya Jivatram Kripalani toured India, speaking actively against her and her government.

State of Emergency (1975-1977)

Gandhi moved to restore order by ordering the arrest of most of the opposition participating in the unrest. Her Cabinet and government then recommended that President Fakhruddin Ali Ahmed declare a state of emergency, because of the disorder and lawlessness following the Allahabad High Court decision.

Accordingly, Ahmed declared a State of Emergency caused by internal disorder, based on the provisions of Article 352 of the Constitution, on 26 June 1975.

Rule by decree

Within a few months, President's Rule was imposed on the two opposition party ruled states of Gujarat and Tamil Nadu thereby bringing the entire country under direct Central rule. Police were granted powers to impose curfews and indefinitely detain citizens and all publications were subjected to substantial censorship by the Ministry of Information and Broadcasting. Inder Kumar Gujral, a future prime minister himself, resigned as Minister for Information and Broadcasting to protest Sanjay Gandhi's interference in his work. Finally, impending legislative assembly elections were indefinitely postponed, with all opposition-controlled state governments being removed by virtue of the constitutional provision allowing for a dismissal of a state government on recommendation of the state's governor.

Indira used the emergency provisions to grant herself extraordinary powers.

"Unlike her father [Nehru], who preferred to deal with strong chief ministers in control of their legislative parties and state party organizations, Mrs. Gandhi set out to remove every Congress chief minister who had an independent base and to replace each of them with ministers personally loyal to her...Even so, stability could not be maintained in the states..."

It is alleged that she further moved President Ahmed to issue ordinances that did not need to be debated in Parliament, allowing her to rule by decree.

Simultaneously, Gandhi's government undertook a campaign to stamp out dissent including the arrest and detention of thousands of political activists; Sanjay was instrumental in initiating the clearing of slums around Delhi's Jama Masjid under the supervision of Jag Mohan, later Lt.

Governor of Delhi, which allegedly left thousands of people homeless and hundreds killed, and led to communal embitterment in those parts of the nation's capital; and the family planning program which forcibly imposed vasectomy on thousands of fathers and was often poorly administered.

ELECTIONS

After extending the state of emergency twice, in 1977 Indira Gandhi called for elections, to give the electorate a chance to vindicate her rule. Gandhi may have grossly misjudged her popularity by reading what the heavily censored press wrote about her. In any case, she was opposed by the Janata Party. Janata, led by her long-time rival, Desai and with Jai Prakash Narayan as its spiritual guide, claimed the elections were the last chance for India to choose between "democracy and dictatorship." Indira's Congress party was beaten soundly. Indira and Sanjay Gandhi both lost their seats, and Congress was cut down to 153 seats (compared with 350 in the previous Lok Sabha), 92 of which were in the south.

CORRUPTION CHARGES

In 1975, Gandhi was found guilty of corruption. Indian Prime Minister Indira Gandhi was barred from holding office for six years after she was found guilty of electoral corruption. But Mrs Gandhi rejected calls to resign and announced plans to appeal to the Supreme Court. The verdict was delivered by Mr Justice Sinha at Allahabad High Court. It came almost four years after the case was brought by Raj Narain, the premier's defeated opponent in the 1971 parliamentary election. Mrs Gandhi, who gave evidence in her defence during the trial, was found guilty of dishonest election practices, excessive election expenditure, and of using government machinery and officials for party purposes. The judge rejected more serious charges of bribery against her.

Indira insisted the conviction did not undermine her position, despite having been unseated from the lower house of parliament, Lok Sabha, by order of the High Court. She said: "There is a lot of talk about our government not being clean, but from our experience the situation was very much worse when [opposition] parties were forming governments". And she dismissed criticism of the way her Congress Party raised election campaign money, saying all parties used the same methods. The prime minister retained the support of her party, which issued a statement backing her. After news of the verdict spread, hundreds of supporters demonstrated outside her house, pledging their loyalty.Indian High Commissioner BK Nehru said Mrs Gandhi's conviction would not harm her political career."Mrs Gandhi has still today overwhelming support in the country," he said. "I believe the prime minister of India will continue in office until the electorate of India decides otherwise".

Indira began an appeal against her conviction for corrupt electoral practices. She controversially declared a state of emergency, claiming there was a plot to disrupt democracy. Thousands were arrested, including about 20 MPs, and the Indian media was censored. In August 1975 the Lok Sabha passed legislation to clear Gandhi of her corruption convictions retroactively, as she had strong-armed her opponents out of Parliament, and had arrested many of them.

REMOVAL, ARREST AND RETURN

Desai became Prime Minister and Neelam Sanjiva Reddy, the establishment choice of 1969, became President of the Republic. Gandhi found herself without work, income or residence until winning a by-election in 1978.

The Congress Party split during the election campaign of 1977. Veteran Gandhi supporter like Jagjivan Ram and her most loyal Bahuguna & Nandini Satpathy parted ways. All three of them were very close to Indira but were compeled due to politicking and circumstances created by Sanjay Gandhi. The rumour then was that Sanjay had intentions of dislodging Indira's power. The Congress (Gandhi) Party was now a much smaller group in Parliament, although the official opposition.

Unable to govern owing to fractious coalition warfare, the Janata government's Home Minister, Choudhary Charan

Singh, ordered the arrest of Indira and Sanjay Gandhi on several charges, none of which would be easy to prove in an Indian court. The arrest meant that Indira was automatically expelled from Parliament. However, this strategy backfired disastrously. Her arrest and long-running trial, however, gained her great sympathy from many people who had feared her as a tyrant just two years earlier.

The Janata coalition was only united by its hatred of Indira (or "that woman" as some called her). With so little in common, the government was bogged down by infighting and Gandhi was able to use the situation to her advantage. She began giving speeches again, tacitly apologizing for "mistakes" made during the Emergency. Desai resigned in June 1979, and Charan Singh was appointed Prime Minister by Reddy after Mrs. Gandhi promised that Congress would support his government from outside.

After a short interval, she withdrew her initial support and President Reddy dissolved Parliament in the winter of 1979. In elections held the following January, Congress was returned to power with a landslide majority. In the 1980s, the Indira Gandhi Government provided money, weapons and military training to LTTE and other Tamil millitant groups in Sri Lanka.

CURRENCY CRISIS

During the early 1980s, Indira's administration failed to arrest the 40 percent fall in the value of the Indian Rupee from 7 to 12 to the US Dollar.

OPERATION BLUE STAR AND ASSASSINATION

Indira Gandhi's blood-stained saree and her belongings at the time of her assassination, preserved at the Indira Gandhi Memorial Museum in New Delhi. In June 1984, Jarnail Singh Bhindranwale's separatist Sikh freedom fighter group was camping within the walls of Golden Temple, Sikhism's holiest shrine. Despite the presence of thousands of civilians in the Golden Temple complex at the time; the army opened fire resulting in civilian casualties. This attempt of Gandhi was highly condemned by international media.

Government and independent accounts differ in the number of military and civilian casualties. Government estimates include four officers, seventy-nine soldiers, and 492 sikhs; independent accounts are much higher, perhaps 500 or more troops and 3, 000 sikhs, including many women and children caught in the crossfire. While the exact figures related to civilian casualties are disputed, lack of decent records, the timing and method of the attack were widely criticized. Most of the criticism was directed was against Indira Gandhi using this as a personal attack on Sikhs. She justified this up by saying the attack was led to flush out terrorist Bhindaranwale who was creating "animosity" by preaching ideas of independence for sikhs, and idea of forming a seperate state called Khalistan.

Indira Gandhi had numerous bodyguards, two of whom were Satwant Singh and Beant Singh, both Sikhs. On 31 October 1984 they assassinated Indira Gandhi with their service weapons in the garden of the Prime Minister's Residence at No. 1, Safdarjung Road in New Delhi. As she was walking to be interviewed by the British actor Peter Ustinov filming a documentary for Irish television, she passed a wicket gate, guarded by Satwant and Beant. According to information available immediately following the incident, Beant Singh shot her three times using his side-arm and Satwant Singh fired twenty-two rounds, using a Sten submachine gun. Beant Singh was shot dead and Satwant Singh was shot and arrested by her other bodyguards.

Indira died on her way to the hospital, in her official car, but she was not declared dead until many hours later. She was taken to the All India Institute of Medical Sciences, where doctors operated on her. Official accounts at the time stated as many as 29 entry and exit wounds and some reports stated 31 bullets were extracted from her body. She was cremated on 3 November, near Raj Ghat. After her death, sectarian unrest created by congress politicians loyal to Indira Gandhi engulfed New Delhi and several other cities in India, including Kanpur, Asansol and Indore, leading to the torture and murder of thousands of Sikhs by the some miscreants.[citation needed] Gandhi's friend and biographer Pupul Jayakar would later reveal Indira's tension, and her premonition about what might happen in the wake of Operation Blue Star.

PERSONAL LIFE

Initially Sanjay had been her chosen heir; but after his death in a flying accident, his mother persuaded a reluctant Rajiv Gandhi to quit his job as a pilot and enter politics in February 1981. After Indira Gandhi's death, Rajiv Gandhi became Prime Minister. In May 1991, he too was assassinated, this time at the hands of Liberation Tigers of Tamil Eelam militants. Rajiv's widow, Sonia Gandhi, led the United Progressive Alliance to a surprise electoral victory in the 2004 Lok Sabha elections.

Sonia Gandhi declined the opportunity to assume the office of Prime Minister but remains in control of the Congress' political apparatus; Prime Minister Dr. Manmohan Singh, formerly finance minister, now heads the nation. Rajiv's children, Rahul Gandhi and Priyanka Gandhi Vadra, have also entered politics. Sanjay Gandhi's widow, Maneka Gandhi - who fell out with Indira after Sanjay's death and was famously thrown out of the Prime Minister's house - as well as Sanjay's son, Varun Gandhi, are active in politics as members of the main opposition BJP party.

INDIRA GANDHI IN POPULAR CULTURE

Her assassination is mentioned by Tom Clancy in his novel *Executive Orders*. Although never mentioned by name, Indira Gandhi is clearly the prime minister in *A Fine Balance* by Rohinton Mistry. In Salman Rushdie's novel *Midnight's Children*, Indira is responsible for the eponymous characters' downfall, referred to throughout the novel as "The Widow." This portrayal of Indira Gandhi raised controversy in some circles for its harsh depiction both of her and of her policies.

In Shashi Tharoor's *The Great Indian Novel,* the character of Priya Duryodhani clearly refers to Indira Gandhi. *Aandhi,* a Hindi feature film directed by Gulzar, is a partly fictionalized adaptation of some events in Indira's life, particularly her (played by Suchitra Sen) difficult relationship with her husband (played by Sanjeev Kumar).

In Yann Martel's *Life of Pi,* Indira Gandhi is noted several times as "Mrs. Gandhi" when referring to the political climate of India in the mid 1970s.

CONTROVERSIES

Indira Gandhi, late Prime Minister of India, implemented a forced sterilization programme in the 1970s.Officially, men with two children or more had to submit to sterilization, but many unmarried young men, political opponents and ignorant men were also believed to have been sterilized. This program is still remembered and criticized in India, and is blamed for creating a wrong public aversion to family planning, which hampered Government programmes for decades.

BENAZIR BHUTTO

Benazir Bhutto (21 June 1953 – 27 December 2007) was a Pakistani politician who chaired the Pakistan Peoples Party (PPP), a centre-left political party in Pakistan. Bhutto was the first woman elected to lead a Muslim state, having twice been Prime Minister of Pakistan (1988–1990; 1993–1996). She was Pakistan's first and to date only female prime minister. Her family is from the Bhutto tribe of Sindhis. Bhutto was the eldest child of former Prime Minister Zulfikar Ali Bhutto, a Pakistani of Sindhi descent and Shia Muslim by faith, and Begum Nusrat Bhutto, a Pakistani of Iranian-Kurdish descent, similarly Shia Muslim by faith. Her paternal grandfather was Sir Shah Nawaz Bhutto, who came to Larkana District in Sindh before the independence from his native town of Bhatto Kalan, in the Indian state of Haryana.

Bhutto was sworn in as Prime Minister for the first time in 1988 at the age of 35, but was removed from office 20 months later under the order of then-president Ghulam Ishaq Khan on grounds of alleged corruption. In 1993 she was re-elected but was again removed in 1996 on similar charges, this time by President Farooq Leghari. She went into self-imposed exile in Dubai in 1998.

Bhutto returned to Pakistan on 18 October 2007, after reaching an understanding with President Pervez Musharraf by which she was granted amnesty and all corruption charges were withdrawn. She was assassinated on 27 December 2007, after departing a PPP rally in the Pakistani city of Rawalpindi, two weeks before the scheduled Pakistani general election of 2008 where she was a leading opposition candidate. The following year she was named one of seven winners of the United Nations Prize in the Field of Human Rights.

EDUCATION AND PERSONAL LIFE

Benazir Bhutto was born in Karachi, Dominion of Pakistan on 21 June 1953 to Begum Nusrat Ispahani and Zulfikar Ali Bhutto of a prominent Muslim family of Larkana. She attended the Lady Jennings Nursery School and Convent of Jesus and Mary in Karachi. After two years of schooling at the Rawalpindi Presentation Convent, she was sent to the Jesus and Mary Convent at Murree. She passed her O-level examinations at the age of 15. She then went on to complete her A-Levels at the Karachi Grammar School.

After completing her early education in Pakistan, she pursued her higher education in the United States. From 1969 to 1973 she attended Radcliffe College at Harvard University, where she obtained a Bachelor of Arts degree with cum laude honors comparative government. She was also elected to Phi Beta Kappa. Bhutto would later call her time at Harvard "four of the happiest years of my life" and said it formed "the very basis of her belief in democracy". Later in 1995 as Prime Minister, she would arrange a gift from the Pakistani government to Harvard Law School. On June 2006, she received an Honorary LL.D degree from the University of Toronto.

The next phase of her education took place in the United Kingdom. Between 1973 and 1977 Bhutto studied Philosophy, Politics, and Economics at Lady Margaret Hall, Oxford, during which time she completed additional courses in International Law and Diplomacy. After LMH she attends St Catherine's College, Oxford and in December 1976 she was elected president of the Oxford Union, becoming the first Asian woman to head the prestigious debating society.

On 18 December 1987, she married Asif Ali Zardari in Karachi. The couple had three children: Bilawal, Bakhtwar and Aseefa.

FAMILY

Benazir Bhutto's father, Prime Minister Zulfikar Ali Bhutto, was removed from office following a military coup in 1977 led by the then chief of army General Muhammad Zia-ul-Haq, who imposed martial law but promised to hold elections within three months. Nevertheless, instead of fulfilling the promise of holding general elections, General Zia charged Mr. Bhutto with conspiring to murder the father of dissident politician Ahmed Raza Kasuri. Mr. Zulfikar Ali Bhutto was sentenced to death by the martial law court. Despite the accusation being "widely doubted by the public", and many clemency appeals from foreign leaders, Zulfikar Ali Bhutto was hanged on 4 April 1979. Appeals for clemency were dismissed by acting President General Zia. Benazir Bhutto and her mother were held in a "police camp" until the end of May, after the execution. In 1985, Benazir Bhutto's brother Shahnawaz was killed under suspicious circumstances in France. Later in 1996 the killing of her other brother, Mir Murtaza, contributed to destabilizing her second term as Prime Minister.

PRIME MINISTER

At left during Parliamentary session in 1998-1999. From left: Chaudhry Muhammad Barjees Tahir, Ajmal Khattak, Aitzaz Ahsan, and Benazir Bhutto.

Bhutto, who had returned to Pakistan after completing her studies, found herself placed under house arrest in the wake of her father's imprisonment and subsequent execution. Having been allowed in 1984 to return to the United Kingdom, she became a leader in exile of the PPP, her father's party, though she was unable to make her political presence felt in Pakistan until after the death of General Muhammad Zia-ul-Haq. She had succeeded her mother as leader of the PPP and the pro-democracy opposition to the Zia-ul-Haq regime.

The seat, from which Benazir contested for the post of Prime Minister, was the same one from which her father had previously contested, namely, NA 207. This seat was first contested in 1926 by the late Sardar Wahid Bux Bhutto, in the first ever elections in Sindh. The elections were for the Central Legislative Assembly of India. Sardar Wahid Bux won, and became not only the first elected representative from Sindh to a democratically elected parliament, but also the youngest member of the Central Legislative Assembly, aged 27. Wahid Bux's achievement was monumental as it was he who was the first Bhutto elected to a government, from a seat which would, thereafter always be contested by his family members.

Therefore, it was he who provided the breakthrough and a start to this cycle. Sardar Wahid Bux went on to be elected to the Bombay Council as well. After Wahid Bux's untimely and mysterious death at the age of 33, his younger brother Nawab Nabi Bux Bhutto contested from the same seat and remained undefeated until retirement. It was he who then gave this seat to Zulfikar Ali Bhutto to contest.

On 16 November 1988, in the first open election in more than a decade, Bhutto's PPP won the largest bloc of seats in the National Assembly. Bhutto was sworn in as Prime Minister of a coalition government on December 2, becoming at age 35 the youngest person-and the first woman to head the government of a Muslim-majority state in modern times. In 1989, Benazir was awarded the Prize for Freedom by the Liberal International. Bhutto's accomplishments during this time were in initiatives for nationalist reform and modernization that some conservatives characterized as Westernization. Bhutto's government was dismissed in 1990 following charges of corruption, for which she was never tried. Zia's protégé Nawaz Sharif came to power after the October 1990 elections. She served as leader of the opposition while Sharif served as Prime Minister for the next three years.

In October 1993 elections were held again and her PPP coalition was victorious, returning Bhutto to office and allowing her to continue her reform initiatives. According to journalist Shyam Bhatia, Bhutto smuggled CDs containing uranium enrichment data to North Korea on a state visit that same year in return for data on missile technology. In 1996, amidst various corruption scandals Bhutto was dismissed by then-president Farooq Leghari, who used the Eighth Amendment discretionary powers to dissolve the government. The Supreme Court affirmed President Leghari's dismissal in a 6-1 ruling. Criticism against Bhutto came from the Punjabi elites and powerful landlord families who opposed Bhutto. She blamed this opposition for the destabilization of Pakistan. Musharraf characterized Bhutto's terms as an "era of sham democracy" and others characterized her terms a period of corrupt, failed governments.

POLICIES FOR WOMEN

During the election campaigns the Bhutto government voiced its concern for women's social and health issues, including the issue of discrimination against women. Bhutto announced plans to establish women's police stations, courts, and women's development banks. Despite these plans, Bhutto did not propose any legislation to improve welfare services for women. During her election campaigns, she promised to repeal controversial laws (such as Hudood and Zina ordinances) that curtail the rights of women in Pakistan. Bhutto was pro-life and spoke forcefully against abortion, most notably at the International Conference on Population and Development in Cairo, where she accused the West of "seeking to impose adultery, abortion, intercourse education and other such matters on individuals, societies and religions which have their own social ethos."

The Zina ordinance was finally repealed by a Presidential Ordinance issued by Pervez Musharraf in July 2006.

Bhutto was an active and founding member of the Council of Women World Leaders, a network of current and former prime ministers and presidents.

POLICY ON TALIBAN

The Taliban took power in Kabul in September 1996. It was during Bhutto's rule that the Taliban gained prominence in Afghanistan. She, like many leaders at the time, viewed the Taliban as a group that could stabilize Afghanistan and enable trade access to the Central Asian republics, according to author Stephen Coll. He claims that like the United States, her government provided military and financial support for the Taliban, even sending a small unit of the Pakistani army into Afghanistan.

More recently, she took an anti-Taliban stance, and condemned terrorist acts allegedly committed by the Taliban and their supporters.

CHARGES OF CORRUPTION

French, Polish, Spanish, and Swiss documents have fuelled the charges of corruption against Bhutto and her husband. They faced a number of legal proceedings, including a charge of laundering money through Swiss banks. Though never convicted, her husband, Asif Ali Zardari, spent eight years in prison on similar corruption charges. After being released on bail in 2004, Zardari suggested that his time in prison involved torture; human rights groups have supported his claim that his rights were violated.

A 1998 *New York Times* investigative report claims that Pakistani investigators have documents that uncover a network of bank accounts, all linked to the family's lawyer in Switzerland, with Asif Zardari as the principal shareholder. According to the article, documents released by the French authorities indicated that Zardari offered exclusive rights to Dassault, a French aircraft manufacturer, to replace the air force's fighter jets in exchange for a 5% commission to be paid to a Swiss corporation controlled by Zardari. The article also said a Dubai company received an exclusive license to import gold into Pakistan for which Asif Zardari received payments of more than $10 million into his Dubai-based Citibank accounts. The owner of the company denied that he had made payments to Zardari and claims the documents were forged.

Bhutto maintained that the charges levelled against her and her husband were purely political. An Auditor General of Pakistan (AGP) report supports Bhutto's claim. It presents information suggesting that Benazir Bhutto was ousted from power in 1990 as a result of a witch hunt approved by then-president Ghulam Ishaq Khan. The AGP report says Khan illegally paid legal advisers 28 million rupees to file 19 corruption cases against Bhutto and her husband in 1990–92.

Yet the assets held by Bhutto and her husband continues to be scrutinized and speculated about. The prosecutors have alleged that their Swiss bank accounts contain £740 million. Zardari also bought a neo-Tudor mansion and estate worth over £4 million in Surrey, England, UK. The Pakistani investigations have tied other overseas properties to Zardari's family. These include a $2.5 million manor in Normandy owned by Zardari's parents, who had modest assets at the time of his marriage. Bhutto denied holding substantive overseas assets.

Switzerland

On 23 July 1998, the Swiss Government handed over documents to the government of Pakistan which relate to corruption allegations against Benazir Bhutto and her husband. The documents included a formal charge of money laundering by Swiss authorities against Zardari. The Pakistani government had been conducting a wide-ranging inquiry to account for more than $13.7 million frozen by Swiss authorities in 1997 that was allegedly stashed in banks by Bhutto and her husband. The Pakistani government recently filed criminal charges against Bhutto in an effort to track down an estimated $1.5 billion she and her husband are alleged to have received in a variety of criminal enterprises. The documents suggest that the money Zardari was alleged to have laundered was accessible to Benazir Bhutto and had been used to buy a diamond necklace for over $175,000. The PPP has responded by flatly denying the charges, suggesting that Swiss authorities have been misled by false evidence provided by the Government of Pakistan.

On 6 August 2003, Swiss magistrates found Bhutto and her husband guilty of money laundering. They were given six-month suspended jail terms, fined $50,000 each and were ordered to pay $11 million to the Pakistani government. The six-year trial concluded that Bhutto and Zardari deposited in Swiss accounts $10 million given to them by a Swiss company in exchange for a contract in Pakistan. The couple said they would appeal. The Pakistani investigators say Zardari opened a Citibank account in Geneva in 1995 through which they say he passed some $40 million of the $100 million he received in payoffs from foreign companies doing business in Pakistan. In October 2007, Daniel Zappelli, chief prosecutor of the canton of Geneva, said he received the conclusions of a money laundering investigation against former Pakistani Prime Minister Benazir Bhutto on October 29, but it was unclear whether there would be any further legal action against her in Switzerland.

Poland

The Polish Government has given Pakistan 500 pages of documentation relating to corruption allegations against Benazir Bhutto and her husband. These charges are in regard to the purchase of 8,000 tractors in a 1997 deal. According to Pakistani officials, the Polish papers contain details of illegal commissions paid by the tractor company in return for agreeing to their contract. It was alleged that the arrangement "skimmed" Rs 103 mn rupees ($2 million) in kickbacks. "The documentary evidence received from Poland confirms the scheme of kickbacks laid out by Asif Zardari and Benazir

Bhutto in the name of (the) launching of Awami tractor scheme", APP said. Bhutto and Asif Ali Zardari allegedly received a 7.15% commission on the purchase through their front men, Jens Schlegelmilch and Didier Plantin of Dargal S.A., who received about $1.969 million for supplying 5,900 Ursus tractors.

France

Potentially the most lucrative deal alleged in the documents involved the effort by Dassault Aviation, a French military contractor. French authorities indicated in 1998 that Bhutto's husband, Zardari, offered exclusive rights to Dassault to replace the air force's fighter jets in exchange for a five percent commission to be paid to a corporation in Switzerland controlled by Zardari.

At the time, French corruption laws forbade bribery of French officials but permitted payoffs to foreign officials, and even made the payoffs tax-deductible in France. However, France changed this law in 2000.

Helicopter scandal

In 1998-1999, an enquiry was conducted by the Public Accounts Committee (PAC) of the Parliament to investigate the matter regarding the purchase of the helicopter. The case involves defrauding substantive sum of $2.168 million and $1.1 million public money.

The record shows that the case was not pursued properly nor diligently. FIR No 1 of 1998 was registered with Federal Investigation Agency State Bank Circle Rawalpindi on the complaint of Cabinet Division. Thorough investigation was conducted by the committee headed by Chaudhry Muhammad Barjees Tahir and two other members, namely Faridullah Jamali and Jamshaid Ali Shah.

During this investigation the committee Chairman Barjees Tahir summoned both the former President Farooq Leghari and former Prime Minister Benazir Bhutto along with others, and they were investigated. The case received extensive media coverage both inside and outside Pakistan. The recommendations of the committee, obtained from the file, are as follows:

6.1: That FIR be lodged against (1) Malik Allah Yar Khan of Kalabagh, (2) Zia Pervez Hussain, (3) and Dr M.A. Khan, and that criminal proceedings be instituted against them for defrauding the government.

6.2: That the amount of $2.168 million be recovered from Malik Allah Yar Khan, Zia Pervez Hussain and Dr M.A. Khan by attaching their properties etc in Pakistan or abroad for this purpose. FIA may be directed to take steps to recover this money through Interpol, if necessary. Any banker or foreign national involved in this fraud may also be taken to task by the Federal Investigation Agency.

6.3: That since Benazir Bhutto is clearly responsible for this loss to the exchequer as major decisions in respect of this contract were taken with her approval or direction and passed on to Cabinet Division through former PS PM (Ahmad Sadiq), FIR may be registered against her for causing loss to state by misuse of her authority as PM, and criminal proceedings be initiated.

6.4: That since Farooq Leghari knows that his name has visibly come up in this case, and he has tried to plead innocent; and since it is unimaginable that those operating in this scandal could have easy access to the top bureaucrats like Cabinet Secretary, Principal Secretary to the Prime Minister and even to the Prime Minister herself without the backing and active support of the President, FIR against him must also be registered and criminal proceedings initiated.

6.5: That as for the senior civil servants involved in the case, Ahmad Sadiq former PS PM, Humayun Faiz Rasul, and Sahibzada Imtiaz former Cabinet Secretary, no action can be taken against them at this stage as they already stand retired/superannuated.

The case was further referred to the National Accountability Bureau in 2000-02 but no action was taken.

Western Asia

In the largest single payment investigators have uncovered, a gold bullion dealer in Western Asia was alleged to have deposited at least $10 million into one of Zardari's accounts after the Bhutto government gave him a monopoly on gold imports that sustained Pakistan's jewellery industry. The money was allegedly deposited into Zardari's Citibank account in Dubai. Pakistan's Arabian Sea coast, stretching from Karachi to the border with Iran, has long been a gold smugglers' haven. Until the beginning of Bhutto's second term, the trade, running into hundreds of millions of dollars a year, was unregulated, with slivers of gold called biscuits, and larger weights in bullion, carried on planes and boats that travel between the Persian Gulf and the largely unguarded Pakistani coast.

Shortly after Bhutto returned as prime minister in 1993, a Pakistani bullion trader in Dubai, Abdul Razzak Yaqub, proposed a deal: in return for the exclusive right to import gold, Razzak would help the government regularize the trade. In November 1994, Pakistan's Commerce Ministry wrote to Razzak informing him that he had been granted a license that made him, for at least the next two years, Pakistan's sole authorized gold importer.

In an interview in his office in Dubai, Razzak acknowledged that he had used the license to import more than $500 million in gold into Pakistan, and that he had travelled to Islamabad several times to meet with Bhutto and Zardari. But he denied that there had been any corruption or secret deals. "I have not paid a single cent to Zardari," he said. Razzak claims that someone in Pakistan who wished to destroy his reputation had contrived to have his company wrongly identified as the depositor. "Somebody in the bank has cooperated with my enemies to make false documents," he said.

Bhutto's niece and others have publicly accused Bhutto of complicity in the killing of her brother Murtaza Bhutto in 1996 by uniformed police officers while she was Prime Minister.

EARLY 2000s IN EXILE

In 2002, Pakistani president Pervez Musharraf amended Pakistan's constitution to ban prime ministers from serving more than two terms. This disqualified Bhutto from ever holding the office again. This move was widely considered to be a direct attack on former Prime Ministers Benazir Bhutto and Nawaz Sharif. On 3 August 2003, Bhutto became a member of Minhaj ul Quran International (an international Muslim educational and welfare organization).

While living in Dubai, United Arab Emirates, she cared for her three children and her mother, who was suffering from Alzheimer's disease, traveling to give lectures and keeping in touch with the PPP's supporters. They were reunited with her husband in December 2004 after more than five years. In 2006, Interpol issued a request for the arrest of Bhutto and her husband on corruption charges, at the request of Pakistan. The Bhuttos questioned the legality of the requests in a letter to Interpol. On 27 January 2007, she was invited by the United States to speak to President George W. Bush and Congressional and State Department officials. Bhutto appeared as a panellist on the BBC TV programme Question Time in the UK in March 2007. She has also appeared on BBC current affairs programme Newsnight on several occasions. She rebuffed comments made by Muhammad Ijaz-ul-Haq in May 2007 regarding the knighthood of Salman Rushdie, citing that he was calling for the assassination of foreign citizens.

Bhutto had declared her intention to return to Pakistan within 2007, which she did, in spite of Musharraf's statements of May 2007 about not allowing her to return ahead of the country's general election, due late 2007 or early 2008. It was speculated that she may have been offered the office of Prime Minister again.

Arthur Herman, a US historian, in a controversial letter published in The Wall Street Journal on 14 June 2007, in response to an article by Bhutto highly critical of the president and his policies, described her as "One of the most incompetent leaders in the history of South Asia", and asserted that she and other elites in Pakistan hate Musharraf because he was a muhajir, the son of one of millions of Indian Muslims who fled to Pakistan during independence in 1947. Herman claimed, "Although it was muhajirs who agitated for the creation of Pakistan in the first place, many native Pakistanis view them with contempt and treat them as third-class citizens."

Nonetheless, by mid-2007, the US appeared to be pushing for a deal in which Musharraf would remain as president but step down as military head, and either Bhutto or one of her nominees would become prime minister.

On 11 July 2007, the Associated Press, in an article about the possible aftermath of the Red Mosque incident, wrote:

Benazir Bhutto, the former prime minister and opposition leader expected by many to return from exile and join Musharraf in a power-sharing deal after year-end general elections, praised him for taking a tough line on the Red Mosque. "I'm glad there was no cease-fire with the militants in the mosque because cease-fires simply embolden the militants," she told Britain's Sky TV on Tuesday. "There will be a backlash, but at some time we have to stop appeasing the militants."

This remark about the Red Mosque was seen with dismay in Pakistan as reportedly hundreds of young students were burned to death and remains are untraceable and cases are being heard in Pakistani Supreme Court as a missing person's issue. This and subsequent support for Musharraf led Elder Bhutto's comrades like Khar to criticize her publicly.

Bhutto however advised Musharraf in an early phase of the latter's quarrel with the Chief Justice, to restore him. Her PPP did not capitalize on its CEC member, Aitzaz Ahsan, the chief Barrister for the Chief Justice, in successful restoration. Rather he was seen as a rival and was isolated.

2002 ELECTION

The Bhutto-led PPP secured the highest number of votes (28.42%) and eighty seats (23.16%) in the national assembly in the October 2002 general elections. Pakistan Muslim League (N) (PML-N) managed to win eighteen seats only. Some of the elected candidates of PPP formed a faction of their own, calling it PPP-Patriots which was being led by Makhdoom Faisal Saleh Hayat, the former leader of Bhutto-led PPP. They later formed a coalition government with Musharraf's party, PML-Q.

RETURN TO PAKISTAN

In mid-2002 Musharraf implemented a two-term limit on Prime Ministers. Both Bhutto and Musharraf's other chief rival, Nawaz Sharif, have already served two terms as Prime Minister. Musharraf's allies in parliament, especially the PMLQ, are unlikely to reverse the changes to allow Prime Ministers to seek third terms, nor to make particular exceptions for either Bhutto or Sharif.

In July 2007, some of Bhutto's frozen funds were released. Bhutto continued to face significant charges of corruption. In an 8 August 2007 interview with the Canadian Broadcasting Corporation, Bhutto revealed the meeting focused on her desire to return to Pakistan for the 2008 elections, and of Musharraf retaining the Presidency with Bhutto as Prime Minister. On 29 August 2007, Bhutto announced that Musharraf would step down as chief of the army. On September 1, 2007, Bhutto vowed to return to Pakistan "very soon", regardless of whether or not she reached a power-sharing deal with Musharraf before then.

On September 17, 2007, Bhutto accused Musharraf's allies of pushing Pakistan into crisis by their refusal to permit democratic reforms and power-sharing.

A nine-member panel of Supreme Court judges deliberated on six petitions (including one from Jamaat-e-Islami, Pakistan's largest Islamic group) asserting that Musharraf be disqualified from contending for the presidency of Pakistan. Bhutto stated that her party could join one of the opposition groups, potentially that of Nawaz Sharif. Attorney-general Malik Mohammed Qayyum stated that, pendente lite; the Election Commission was "reluctant" to announce the schedule for the presidential vote. Bhutto's party's Farhatullah Babar stated that the Constitution of Pakistan could bar Musharraf from being elected again because he was already Chief of the army: "As Gen. Musharraf was disqualified from contesting for President, he has prevailed upon the Election Commission to arbitrarily and illegally tamper with the Constitution of Pakistan."

Musharraf prepared to switch to a strictly civilian role by resigning from his position as commander-in-chief of the armed forces. He still faced other legal obstacles to running for re-election. On 2 October 2007, Gen. Musharraf named Lt. Gen. Ashfaq Kayani, as vice chief of the army starting October 8 with the intent that if Musharraf won the presidency and resigned his military post, Kayani would become chief of the army. Meanwhile, Minister Sheikh Rashid Ahmed stated that officials agreed to grant Benazir Bhutto amnesty versus pending corruption charges. She has emphasized the smooth transition and returns to civilian rule and has asked Pervez Musharraf to shed uniform. On 5 October 2007, Musharraf signed the National Reconciliation Ordinance, giving amnesty to Bhutto and other political leaders except exiled former premier Nawaz Sharif-in all court cases against them, including all corruption charges.

The Ordinance came a day before Musharraf faced the crucial presidential poll. Bhutto's opposition party, the PPP, and the ruling PMLQ, were involved in negotiations beforehand about the deal. In return, Bhutto and the PPP agreed not to boycott the Presidential election. On 6 October 2007, Musharraf won a parliamentary election for President.

However, the Supreme Court ruled that no winner can be officially proclaimed until it finishes deciding on whether it was legal for Musharraf to run for President while remaining Army General. Bhutto's PPP party did not join the other opposition parties' boycott of the election, but did abstain from voting. Later, Bhutto demanded security coverage on-par with the President's. Bhutto also contracted foreign security firms for her protection.

RETURN

Bhutto was well aware of the risk to her own life that might result from her return from exile to campaign for the leadership position. In an interview on September 28, 2007, with reporter Wolf Blitzer of CNN, she readily admitted the possibility of attack on herself. After eight years in exile in Dubai and London, Bhutto returned to Karachi on 18 October 2007, to prepare for the 2008 national elections.

En route to a rally in Karachi on 18 October 2007 two explosions occurred shortly after Bhutto had landed and left Jinnah International Airport. She was not injured but the explosions, later found to be a suicide-bomb attack, killed 136 people and injured at least 450. The dead included at least 50 of the security guards from her PPP who had formed a human chain around her truck to keep potential bombers away, as well as six police officers. A number of senior officials were injured. Bhutto, after nearly ten hours of the parade through Karachi, ducked back down into the steel command center to remove her sandals from her swollen feet, moments before the bomb went off. She was escorted unharmed from the scene.

Bhutto later claimed that she had warned the Pakistani government that suicide bomb squads would target her upon her return to Pakistan and that the government had failed to act. She was careful not to blame Pervez Musharraf for the attacks, accusing instead "certain individuals within the government who abuse their positions, who abuse their powers" to advance the cause of Islamic militants. Shortly after the attempt on her life, Bhutto wrote a letter to Musharraf naming four persons whom she suspected of carrying out the attack. Those named included Chaudhry Pervaiz Elahi, a rival PML-Q politician and chief minister of Pakistan's Punjab province, Hamid Gul, former director of the Inter-Services Intelligence, and Ijaz Shah, the director general of the Intelligence Bureau, another of the country's intelligence agencies.

All those named are close associates of General Musharraf. Bhutto has a long history of accusing parts of the government, particularly Pakistan's premier military intelligence agencies, of working against her and her party because they oppose her liberal, secular agenda. Bhutto claimed that the ISI has for decades backed militant Islamic groups in Kashmir and in Afghanistan. She was protected by her vehicle and a "human cordon" of supporters who had anticipated suicide attacks and formed a chain around her to prevent potential bombers from getting near her. The total number of injured, according to PPP sources, stood at 1000, with at least 160 dead (The New York Times claims 134 dead and about 450 injured). A few days later, Bhutto's lawyer Senator Farooq H. Naik said he received a letter threatening to kill his client.

2007 STATE OF EMERGENCY AND RESPONSE

On 3 November 2007, President Pervez Musharraf declared a state of emergency, citing actions by the Supreme Court of Pakistan and religious extremism in the nation. Bhutto returned to the country, interrupting a visit to family in Dubai. She was greeted by supporters chanting slogans at the airport. After staying in her plane for several hours she was driven to her home in Lahore, accompanied by hundreds of supporters. While acknowledging that Pakistan faced a political crisis, she noted that Musharraf's declaration of emergency, unless lifted, would make it very difficult to have fair elections. She commented that "The extremists need a dictatorship, and dictatorship needs extremists." On 8 November 2007, Bhutto was placed under house arrest just a few hours before she was due to lead and address a rally against the state of emergency.

The following day, the Pakistani government announced that Bhutto's arrest warrant had been withdrawn and that she would be free to travel and to appear at public rallies. However, leaders of other opposition political parties remained prohibited from speaking in public.

PREPARATION FOR 2008 ELECTIONS

On 24 November 2007, Bhutto filed her nomination papers for January's Parliamentary elections; two days later, she filed papers in the Larkana constituency for two regular seats. She did so as former Pakistani Prime Minister Nawaz Sharif, following seven years of exile in Saudi Arabia, made his much-contested return to Pakistan and bid for candidacy. When sworn in again on 30 November 2007, this time as a civilian president after relinquishing his post as military chief, Musharraf announced his plan to lift the Pakistan's state of emergency rule on December 16. Bhutto welcomed the announcement and launched a manifesto outlining her party's domestic issues. Bhutto told journalists in Islamabad that her party, the PPP, would focus on "the five E's": employment, education, energy, environment, equality.

On 4 December 2007, Bhutto met with Nawaz Sharif to publicize their demand that Musharraf fulfill his promise to lift the state of emergency before January's parliamentary elections, threatening to boycott the vote if he failed to comply. They promised to assemble a committee which would present to Musharraf the list of demands upon which their participation in the election was contingent. On 8 December 2007, three unidentified gunmen stormed Bhutto's PPP office in the southern western province of Baluchistan. Three of Bhutto's supporters were killed.

ASSASSINATION

On 27 December 2007 (one day after boxing day, 3rd anniversary after 2004 Indian Ocean earthquake), Bhutto was killed while leaving a campaign rally for the PPP at Liaquat National Bagh, where she had given a spirited address to party supporters in the run-up to the January 2008 parliamentary elections. After entering her bulletproof vehicle, Bhutto stood up through its sunroof to wave to the crowds. At this point, a gunman fired shots at her and subsequently explosives were detonated near the vehicle killing approximately 20 people. Bhutto was critically wounded and was rushed to Rawalpindi General Hospital. She was taken into surgery at 17:35 local time, and pronounced dead at 18:16.

Bhutto's body was flown to her hometown of Garhi Khuda Bakhsh in Larkana District, Sindh, and was buried next to her father in the family mausoleum at a ceremony attended by hundreds of thousands of mourners.

There was some disagreement about the exact cause of death. Bhutto's husband refused to permit an autopsy or post-mortem examination to be carried out. On 28 December 2007, the Interior Ministry of Pakistan stated that "Bhutto was killed when she tried to duck back into the vehicle, and the shock waves from the blast knocked her head into a lever attached to the sunroof, fracturing her skull". However, a hospital spokesman stated earlier that she had suffered shrapnel wounds to the head and that this was the cause of her death. Bhutto's aides have also disputed the Interior Ministry's account. On December 31, CNN posted the alleged emergency room admission report as a PDF file. The document appears to have been signed by all the admitting physicians and notes that no object was found inside the wound.

Al-Qaeda commander Mustafa Abu al-Yazid claimed responsibility for the attack, describing Bhutto as "the most precious American asset." The Pakistani government also stated that it had proof that al-Qaeda was behind the assassination. A report for CNN stated: "the Interior Ministry also earlier told Pakistan's Geo TV that the suicide bomber belonged to Lashkar i Jhangvi-an al-Qaeda-linked militant group that the government has blamed for hundreds of killings". The government of Pakistan claimed Baitullah Mehsud was the mastermind behind the assassination. Lashkar i Jhangvi, a Wahabi Muslim extremist organization affiliated with al-Qaeda that also attempted in 1999 to assassinate former Prime Minister Nawaz Sharif, is alleged to have been responsible for the killing of the 54-year-old Bhutto along with approximately 20 bystanders, however this is vigorously disputed by the Bhutto family, by the PPP that Bhutto had headed and by Baitullah Mehsud. On 3 January 2008, President Musharraf officially denied participating in the assassination of Benazir Bhutto as well as failing to provide her proper security.

REACTION IN PAKISTAN

After the assassination, there were initially a number of riots resulting in approximately 20 deaths, of which three were of police officers. Around 250 cars were burnt; angry and upset supporters of Bhutto threw rocks outside the hospital where she was being held. Through December 29, 2007, the Pakistani government said rioters had wrecked nine election offices, 176 banks, 34 gas stations, 72 train cars, 18 rail stations, and hundreds of cars and shops. Nawaz Sharif, the leader of the rival opposition party Pakistan Muslim League (N), stated that "This is a tragedy for her party and a tragedy for our party and the entire nation." President Musharraf decreed a three-day period of mourning.

On 30 December 2007, at a news conference following a meeting of the PPP leadership, Bhutto's widower Asif Ali Zardari and son Bilawal Bhutto Zardari announced that 19-year-old Bilawal will succeed his mother as titular head of the party, with his father effectively running the party until his son completes his studies at Christ Church, Oxford. "When I return, I promise to lead the party as my mother wanted me to," Bilawal said. The PPP called for parliamentary elections to take place as scheduled on 8 January 2008, and Asif Ali Zardari said that vice-chair Makhdoom Amin Fahim would probably be the party's candidate for prime minister. (Bilawal is not of legal age to stand for parliament.)

On December 30, Bhutto's political party, the Pakistan Peoples Party (PPP), called for the UK Government and the

United Nations to help conduct the investigation of her death. Bilawal Bhutto Zardari has been appointed chairman of his late mother's opposition political party in Pakistan. Bilawal is only 19 years old. On 5 February 2008, the PPP released Mrs. Bhutto's political will which she wrote two weeks before returning to Pakistan and only 12 weeks before she was killed, stating that her husband Asif Ali Zardari would be the leader of the party, until a new leader is elected.

INTERNATIONAL REACTION

The international reaction to Bhutto's assassination was of strong condemnation across the international community. The UN Security Council held an emergency meeting and unanimously condemned the assassination. Arab League Secretary General Amr Moussa stated that, "We condemn this assassination and terrorist act, and pray for God Almighty to bless her soul." India's Prime Minister Manmohan Singh said he was "deeply shocked and horrified to hear of the heinous assassination of Mrs. Benazir Bhutto.... My heartfelt condolences go to her family and the people of Pakistan who have suffered a grievous blow." British Prime Minister Gordon Brown stated, "Benazir Bhutto may have been killed by terrorists but the terrorists must not be allowed to kill democracy in Pakistan and this atrocity strengthens our resolve that terrorists will not win there, here or anywhere in the world."

European Commission President José Manuel Barroso condemned the assassination as "an attack against democracy and against Pakistan," and "hopes that Pakistan will remain firmly on track for return to democratic civilian rule." US President George W. Bush condemned the assassination as a "cowardly act by murderous extremists," and encouraged Pakistan to "honor Benazir Bhutto's memory by continuing with the democratic process for which she so bravely gave her life." Vatican Secretary of State Tarcisio Bertone expressed the sadness of Pope Benedict XVI, saying that "the Holy Father expresses sentiments of deep sympathy and spiritual closeness to the members of her family and to the entire Pakistani nation." Chinese Foreign Ministry spokesperson Qin Gang said that China was "shocked at the killing of Pakistan's opposition leader Benazir Bhutto" and "strongly condemns the terrorist attack."

SCOTLAND YARD INVESTIGATION

British detectives were asked by the Pakistan Government to investigate the assassination. Although expressing reservations as to the difficulty in investigating due to the crime scene having been hosed down and Asif Zardari refuses permission for a *post mortem*, they announced on 8 February 2008 that Benazir Bhutto had been killed by impact with the knob on the sun roof following the bomb explosion.

FILM ON THE LIFE OF BENAZIR

It has been reported that Bollywood actress Sushmita Sen will portray Benazir Bhutto in a film co-produced by Zaid Aziz and Henna Rai of Karachi production firm Vox Vision and Leicester-based Sum Films respectively. Tentatively titled "Benazir Bhutto: The Movie", the flick will be shot at various locations in Pakistan, the US, Britain and Dubai, where Bhutto had spent years as a student and later as a political leader in exile. When asked Sushmita about playing this big role, she excitedly told, "Yes, I am keen to play the role."

ALLEGATION OF GIVING NUCLEAR SECRETS TO NORTH KOREA

Shyam Bhatia, an Indian journalist, alleged in his book Goodbye Shahzadi that in 1993, Bhutto had downloaded secretive information on uranium enrichment to give to North Korea in exchange for information on developing ballistic missiles. Bhatia alleges that Bhutto had asked him to not tell the story during her lifetime. Nuclear expert David Albright of the Institute of Science and International Security said the allegations "made sense" given the timeline of North Korea's nuclear development. George Perkovich of the Carnegie Endowment for International Peace called Bhatia a "smart and serious guy." Selig Harrison of the Center for International Policy called Bhatia "credible on Bhutto". The Pakistani Embassy in Washington, D.C. denied the claims and an United States official dismissed them, insisting that Abdul Qadeer Khan, who had been accused of proliferating secrets before to North Korea (only to later deny them prior to Bhatia's book), was the source.

TRIBUTES

The Pakistani government honoured Bhutto on her birth anniversary by renaming the Islamabad International Airport after her. Prime Minister Yousuf Raza Gilani, a member of Bhutto's PPP also asked President Musharraf to pardon convicts on death row on her birthday in honour of Bhutto.

KHALEDA ZIA

Begum Khaleda Zia (born August 15, 1945) is a former Prime Minister of Bangladesh, having served from 1991 to 1996, becoming the first woman in the country's history to hold that position. She served again from 2001 to 2006. Zia is the widow of assassinated President of Bangladesh Ziaur Rahman, and leads his old party, the Bangladesh Nationalist Party (BNP).

After 35 years of independence of Bangladesh she has ruled the country for about 10 years (longest period). She has been elected to five separate parliamentary constituencies in the general elections of 1991, 1996, and 2001, a feat unachieved by any other politician in Bangladeshi history. In 2006, Forbes ranked Khaleda Zia at number 33 in its list of the 100 Most Powerful Women in the world.

EARLY LIFE

Khaleda Zia was born to Iskandar Majumder and Taiyaba Majumder in Dinajpur District on 15 August 1945. The family originally hails from Feni, a southeastern district of the country. She studied in Dinajpur Government Girls High School.In 1960, she married Ziaur Rahman.

FIRST LADY

Her husband later became Chief of the Armed Forces and subsequently assumed power as Chief Martial Law Administrator following a series of military coups. He attempted to move toward a civilian administration by forming the BNP and becoming democratically elected as President.

POLITICAL CAREER

Until the assassination of her husband, President Ziaur Rahman, in an abortive military coup in Chittagong on 30 May 1981, Khaleda Zia had taken little interest in either politics or public life. Even when her husband assumed power after the political changes in 1975, she remained a shy and withdrawn housewife spending most of her time raising her two sons.

After the assassination of President Ziaur Rahman, Vice-President Justice Abdus Sattar took over as the acting President and also as Chairman of the BNP. Army Chief of Staff General Hossain Mohammad Ershad overthrew Justice Sattar on March 24, 1982. In March 1983, Justice Sattar appointed Khaleda Zia as vice-chairman of the BNP. In February 1984, she became the chairperson as Justice Sattar retired from politics. On August 10, 1984 the party elected her the chairperson.

Under the leadership of Begum Zia, the BNP formed a 7-party alliance in 1983 and launched a relentless struggle against the autocratic regime of General Ershad. During the 9-year-long struggle against Ershad, Begum Zia did not compromise with his autocratic and illegitimate government. For her strict adherence to the principles, the government restricted her movements by using prohibitive laws. She was detained seven times in eight years.

But undaunted, Begum Zia continued to provide leadership in the movement for ousting Ershad. Like Zia before him, Ershad attempted to give his rule a civilian and democratic face, but Khaleda Zia boycotted all elections during his rule. Khaleda was detained seven times during almost nine years of autocratic rule under President Ershad before his resignation on 6 December 1990.

In the face of a mass upsurge spearheaded by alliances led by Begum Zia and Sheikh Hasina, Ershad at last handed over power to a neutral caretaker government on December 6, 1990. In the parliamentary elections held under this government on February 27, 1991, Bangladesh Nationalist Party emerged victorious as a single majority party. Begum Zia contested from five constituencies in three consecutive parliamentary elections and won in all seats. This of course, is a unique feat in the history of elections in the country.

Prime Minister

First term

With a unanimous vote cutting across all political lines, the BNP-led government restored the parliamentary system through the 12th amendment to the Constitution in 1991. A neutral caretaker government oversaw elections on February 27, 1991 that were broadly considered to be free, fair and truly democratic. Khaleda Zia became Bangladesh's first female Prime Minister with the support of the majority of the members of the parliament.

While in power, Begum Zia's government made considerable progress in the education sector, including introduction of free and compulsory primary education, tuition-free education for girls up to class ten, stipend for female students and the Food for Education programme. It also goes to the credit of her government that during this period, the tree plantation had become a nationwide social movement. Further, it was in this period that the construction of the Jamuna Bridge was started. Khaleda Zia played a commendable role in revitalising the South Asian Association for Regional Cooperation. It also increased the age limit for entry into the civil service from 27 years to 30 years and made highest budgetary allocation in the education sector.

Second term

She became Prime Minister for the second consecutive term after the BNP had a landslide victory in February 15, 1996 general election to the sixth Jatiya Sangsad. The election was, however, boycotted by all other major parties who were demanding that the elections be held under a neutral caretaker government, following allegations of rigging in a by-election held in 1994.

Turnout was estimated at around 25%, though the government at the time claimed it to be much higher. The short-lived parliament hastily introduced the Caretaker Government through 13th amendment to the Constitution, and then was dissolved to pave the way for the parliamentary elections. In the June 12, 1996 polls, BNP lost to Sheikh Hasina's Awami League but emerged as the largest opposition party in the country's parliamentary history with 116 seats.

Third term

Aiming to return to power, the BNP formed a four-party alliance on January 6, 1999 with its former political foe the Jatiya Party, and the Islamic party of Jamaat-e-Islami Bangladesh and the Islami Oikya Jot and launched several agitation programmes against the ruling Awami League. Khaleda Zia, like Ziaur Rahman has been criticized much for making alliance with Jamaat-e-Islami, the party which opposed the independence of Bangladesh in 1971 and formed Razakar, Al-Badar and Al-Shams team to help West Pakistan to kill thousands of innocent people including the intellectuals of Bangladesh. Around 3 million people were killed by West Pakistan army with the help of Razakars, Al-Badars and Al-Shams in 1971 within 9 months of war.

The four-party alliance then participated in the October 1, 2001 general elections and won the election with a two-third majority of seats in parliament and 46% of the vote (compared to the principal opposition party's 40%) and Khaleda Zia was once again sworn in as the Prime Minister of Bangladesh.

Khaleda Zia's third term was plagued by rising religious militancy, continuing its spiralling of corruption (including successive damning reports by Transparency International), a rise in alleged attacks on minority groups (such as Hindus and Ahmadiyas as documented by the US State Department and Amnesty International) and an increasingly explosive political environment. A particularly controversial piece of legislation introduced by the government was the banning of Ahmadiya publications in January 2004, which attracted considerable concern from international observers.

END OF TERM

On October 27, 2006, Zia's term in office ended. The following day rioting broke out on the streets of central Dhaka following uncertainty over who would succeed her as Chief Advisor (Chief of Caretaker Government). On the same day evening, a presidential statement declared that former Supreme Court chief justice K.M. Hasan (who had been due to take over as Chief Advisor) would not be assuming the role due to ill health. Subsequently, Iajuddin Ahmed, the current president, assumed power as Chief Advisor on October 29.

POLITICAL CONTROVERSIES

After tremendous domestic and international pressure and amid Awami League claims of partisanship, Iajuddin stepped down as head of the caretaker government. Elections scheduled for January 22 were postponed. The new caretaker government, in its fight against corruption, has targeted many of Zia's BNP ministers.

Zia's son, Tareque Rahman, was also arrested in March 2007 for corruption. It was later reported that, beginning on April 9, the government barred other politicians from visiting Zia's residence due to the state of emergency, imposed in January, which prohibits political activity. Another son of Zia, Arafat Rahman Koko aka Coco, was arrested on April 16. Since United News Bangladesh (UNB) carried unverified reports of

Arafat's arrest on April 16, it cited unnamed 'family sources' as claiming Zia was considering exile. UNB said speculation was mounting Zia would relocate to Saudi Arabia. It also noted her brother; Major (Retd) Syeed Eskandar was attempting to negotiate her exit from Bangladesh with authorities from the interim administration. The New Nation newspaper carried a report on April 17 stating Khaleda had in fact agreed to go into exile in return for the release of her youngest son. The report said the Saudi government had expressed its willingness to accept Khaleda and her family members as royal guests. Meanwhile, Bangladesh's The Daily Star quoted an unnamed source who claimed Zia's decision to leave the nation meant authorities would now force Awami League president Sheikh Hasina, Zia's bitter rival who was then in the United States, to also embrace exile. All these reports about exile and government pressure on Zia were denied by the government.

On April 19, Khondker Babul Chowdhury, a member of the BNP national executive committee, filed the appeal urging the court to order the government not to send Khaleda abroad against her wish and challenging the reported confinement of Khaleda to her house. On April 22 the High Court (HC) issued a rule on the government to explain within five days why the court will not direct the government to produce Khaleda Zia before the court to prove that she is not confined to her house. On April 25, in what was viewed as a reversal, the government said that Zia's movement was not restricted and that she had not been under any pressure to leave the country; it also dropped its ban on Hasina's return. On May 7, the government was ordered by the High Court to explain restrictions on Zia that were said to remain in place.

On July 17, the Anti-Corruption Commission sent notices to both Zia and Hasina, requesting that details of their assets be submitted to the Commission within one week. Zia was asked to appear in court on September 27, 2007 in connection with a case for not submitting service returns for Daily Dinkal Publications Limited for years.

On September 2, 2007, a case was filed against Zia by the interim government for corruption regarding the awarding of contracts to Global Agro Trade Company in 2003, and on September 3 she was arrested. Her son Arafat Rahman along with 11 others was also detained after police recorded a corruption case against them involving irregularities at Chittagong port. A bribery case was also filed against ex-prime minister Sheikh Hasina (rival of Khaleda), detained in a special jail. On the same day, Zia expelled party Secretary General Abdul Mannan Bhuiyan and Joint Secretary General Ashraf Hossain for breaching party discipline. On September 30, Zia was granted bail by the High Court, which also ruled that the trial should be stopped on the grounds that the emergency laws could not be applied to her actions before they were imposed in January 2007. The government appealed this decision, however, and on October 4, 2007 the Supreme Court ruled that she should not be granted bail and that the trial should continue.

After Zia was detained, some party members chose Hafizuddin Ahmed to lead the party; Zia's supporters did not recognize this. The electoral commission subsequently invited Hafizuddin's faction, rather than Zia's, to participate in talks, effectively recognizing the former as the legitimate BNP. Zia challenged this in court, but her appeal was rejected on April 10, 2008.

Zia's son Arafat Rahman Koko was released in August 2008 and her son Tareque was released on bail on September 3, 2008. Zia had been granted bail on two of her four cases by this point, but remained in jail because bail had not been granted for the other two. Her lawyers said on September 4 that they would also seek bail for the other two cases.

SHEIKH HASINA

Sheikh Hasina Wazed (Bengali: Shekh Hasina Oajed) (born September 28, 1947) is a Bangladeshi politician and current Prime Minister of Bangladesh. She has been the President of the Awami League, a major political party, since 1981. She is the eldest of five children of Sheikh Mujibur Rahman, the founding father (and first president) of Bangladesh and wife of an international repute nuclear scientist M. A. Wazed Miah. Sheikh Hasina's party defeated the BNP-led Four-Party Alliance in the 2008 parliamentary elections, thus assuring her the post of prime minister. Sheikh Hasina has once before held the office of PM, from 1996 to 2001.

EARLY LIFE

Sheikh Hasina's political career started as a student activist in Eden College in the 1960s. While at Government Intermediate College, she was elected vice president of the College Students Union for the term 1966–67. Her opponent was the leftist student leader Motiya Chowdhury, who much later joined Awami League and became a member of Hasina's cabinet.

At the University of Dhaka Sheikh Hasina was a member of the Chhatra League (the student wing of Awami League) and secretary of the Rokeya Hall unit. During the liberation war in 1971, Hasina, then a young mother, was in-house arrest with her mother, brothers, sister and her son. Sheikh Mujibur Rahman was imprisoned in West Pakistan during this period. After liberation, Hasina's involvement in politics was minimal as Sheikh Kamal, her brother, was touted as Mujib's successor.

MEMBER OF THE NATIONAL ASSEMBLY

Her political and personal destiny was irrevocably altered on the fateful night of August 15, 1975, when her father and almost her entire family including her mother and three brothers were assassinated in a coup d'etat by a section of disgruntled officers of the Bangladesh Army, some of whom were freedom fighters during 1971. Sheikh Hasina and her sister, Sheikh Rehana was on a goodwill tour of West Germany at that time. Hasina then sought refuge in United Kingdom and later, in India. She was exiled to New Delhi, India until May 17, 1981 when she was allowed to return to Bangladesh.

MOVEMENT AGAINST AUTOCRACY

While living in self-exile in India, Sheikh Hasina was elected the president of Bangladesh Awami League in 1981. After she returned to the country, the president Ziaur Rahman was assassinated in yet another coup in May, 1981. The following year, General Hossain Mohammad Ershad captured power through a bloodless coup and declared martial law. In 1983, Hasina formed the 15-party alliance to launch a movement to oust him from power. She was in and out of prison throughout the 1980s. Her party, along with the Bangladesh Nationalist Party, led by Rahman's widow Khaleda Zia, was instrumental in the movement against the military rule. In 1984, Hasina was put under house arrest in February and then again in November. In March 1985, she was put under house arrest for three months. In 1990, Hasina's 8 party alliances was instrumental along with another BNP-led alliance in finally removing the Ershad regime.

Under the leadership of Sheikh Hasina, Awami League formed an alliance with Ershad's Jayiya Party in 2006.

LEADER OF THE OPPOSITION

Sheikh Hasina and her party Awami League participated in the 1986 Parliamentary election held under President Lieutenant General Hossain Mohammad Ershad. She served as the leader of the opposition between 1986-1987. Hasina's decision to partake in the election has been criticized by her opponents, since the election was held under dictatorial rule. Her supporters maintain that she used the platform effectively to challenge Ershad's rule. The parliament was dissolved in December, 1987.

The first democratic elections were held in 1991 after a long period of military rule. A caretaker government, headed by Shahabuddin Ahmed, the outgoing chief justice, oversaw the elections. The Bangladesh Nationalist Party won the election, and Hasina's Awami League emerged as the largest opposition party. Hasina was defeated in the Dhaka constituency that she contested by Sadeque Hossain Khoka, a future Mayor of Dhaka, but was elected to the Parliament from her home constituency in Gopalganj. Hasina accused the BNP of "nuanced rigging" in elections. Hasina nevertheless offered to resign as the party president but later stayed on at the request of party leaders. Khaleda Zia of the BNP took office as the first female Prime Minister of Bangladesh.

Politics in Bangladesh took a decisive turn in 1994, after Magura by-elections. This election was held after the MP for that constituency, a member of Hasina's party, died. The Awami League was expected to win it back, but the seat was won by the BNP. The opposition parties accused the BNP of widespread rigging and the election commission of incompetence. The Awami League, with other opposition parties, demanded that the next election be held under a caretaker government, and that the notion of a caretaker government be incorporated in the constitution. The ruling party of Khaleda Zia, Hasina's arch rival, refused to give in to these demands.

Opposition parties launched an unprecedented campaign, calling strikes for weeks on end. The government accused them of destroying the economy while the opposition countered that BNP could solve this problem by acceding to their demands. In late 1995, the MPs of the Awami League and other parties lost their seats due to prolonged absence from parliament. The government declared elections on February 15, 1996, an election that was boycotted by all major parties except the ruling BNP. Hasina claimed that the election was a farce. The elected parliament, almost totally composed of BNP members, finally amended the constitution to create provisions for a caretaker government. The next parliamentary election was held under a caretaker government headed by Justice Habibur Rahman on June 30, 1996.

PRIME MINISTER

The Awami League won 146 seats in the 1996 parliamentary elections. The support of the Jatiya Party and a few independent candidates were enough for the 150+ seats needed for the required majority. Hasina took the oath as Prime minister of Bangladesh. She vowed to create a Government of National Unity. Though some smaller parties and a few individuals from BNP did join the government, the distance between the main two political parties (as well as their leaders) remained as large as ever. Hasina did manage to convince Justice Shahabuddin Ahmed, who led the first caretaker government, to assume the post of President. This selection of an unbiased person as president was praised by her supporters as a proof of Hasina's good will to reach out to the opposition.

A major achievement of the new government was to strike a treaty between India and Bangladesh concerning the Farakka Barrage, a bone of contention between the two countries ever since it was built in the 1960s. According to the treaty, Bangladesh was to receive 33 thousand cubic feet per second (930 m^3/s) of water. Hasina next went on to create a 'Peace Treaty' with the tribal rebels in the mountainous southeast of the country, thus seemingly solving a problem as old as Bangladesh itself. Though rebel activities have reduced greatly after the treaty, the region remains a hotbed of tensions. US President Bill Clinton and Prime Minister Sheikh Hasina making a joint statement to the press following their bilateral meeting, Prime Minister's office, Bangladesh (March 2000).

On the down side, the Awami League was criticize for harbouring gangsters turned politicians, most notably Jainal Hazari of Feni. Her government was also criticized for overusing Sheikh Mujibur Rahman - the country's founding leader and also father to Sheikh Hasina - in the media and naming many major institutions and constructions after him. The Awami League maintained that previous governments had tried to systematically eradicate Sheikh Mujib's legacy from the country and that the honour he was getting was long overdue. The BNP also accused the Awami League of politicising the administration and state-owned media. Her party was also accused of being lenient towards India, especially after a shootout between border forces of India and Bangladesh left 16 Indian and 3 Bangladeshi border guards dead.

During the last year of her rule, Transparency International declared Bangladesh to be the most corrupt country in the world. Though Bangladesh had almost always been in the bottom five, the last position created uproar and was seen by many as a major failure by Hasina. Though Hasina was voted out of office later, Bangladesh has remained at the last position. The opposition demanded that Hasina resign and declare early elections, but Hasina refused to do so. She became the first democratically elected prime minister to complete her term.

Justice Latifur Rahman became the head of the caretaker government. Awami League alleged that he was biased towards BNP after he transferred a large number of civil servants immediately after taking office. Later, Hasina would also accuse President Shahabuddin Ahmed and election official Abu Sayeed of biased actions.

The Awami League succumbed to a landslide defeat in the 2001 Parliament elections. It won only 62 seats in the Parliament, while the 'Four Party Alliance' led by the Bangladesh Nationalist Party won more than 200 seats, giving them a two-thirds majority in Parliament. Hasina herself was defeated in a constituency in Rangpur, which happened to contain her husband's hometown, but won in two other seats. Sheikh Hasina and the Awami League rejected the results, claiming that the election was rigged with the help of the President and the Caretaker government. However, the international community was largely satisfied with the elections and the 'Four Party Alliance' went on to form the government.

The Awami League has been irregular in the Parliament ever since. Hasina maintains that the ruling party didn't give the opposition enough time on the floor. In late 2003, the Awami League started its first major anti-government movement, culminating in the declaration by party general secretary Abdul

Jalil that the government would fall before April 30, 2004. This failed to happen and was seen as a blow to the party and Hasina herself, who had implicitly supported Jalil.

In her second term in opposition, Hasina has been faced with assassination attempts against herself and killings of important party personnel. Ahsanullah Master, an MP, was killed in 2004. This was followed by a grenade attack on Hasina in Dhaka, resulting in the death of 21 party supporters, including party women's secretary Ivy Rahman. Finally, her ex finance minister Shah M S Kibria was killed in a grenade attack in Sylhet.

In June 2005, the Awami League got a boost when AL-nominated incumbent mayor A.B.M. Mohiuddin Chowdhury won the important mayoral election in Chittagong, the port city and second largest city in Bangladesh. This election was seen as a showdown between the opposition and the ruling party.

The planned January 22, 2007 elections were marred by controversy. The Awami League and its allies protested, saying that the elections would not be fair because of alleged bias by the caretaker government in favor of Zia and the BNP. Hasina demanded that the head of the caretaker government, President Iajuddin Ahmed, step down and on January 3, 2007, she announced that the Awami League and its allies would boycott the elections. Later in the month a state of emergency was imposed, Ahmed stepped down, and the elections were postponed.

EXTORTION ALLEGATIONS AND CRIMINAL CHARGES

On April 9, 2007, it was announced that Bangladesh police were investigating extortion charges against Hasina. She was accused of forcing Bangladeshi businessman Tajul Islam Farooq to pay bribes before his company could build a power plant in 1998. Farooq said that he paid Hasina 30 million takas (US$441,000, or €383,211) to get his project approved by the government, according to a police official.

On April 11, murder charges were filed against her by the police, alleging that she masterminded the killing of four supporters of a rival political party in October 2006. The four alleged victims were beaten to death during clashes between the Awami League and rival party activists. Deputy police commissioner, Shahidul Haq Bhuiyan said "detective branch police submitted the charge-sheet of the case to a Dhaka court today after carrying out investigations and taking evidence." She was visiting the United States at the time.

The interim administration subsequently took steps to prevent Hasina's return to Bangladesh, with The New Nation newspaper reporting on April 17 that airlines had been asked not to allow her to return to Dhaka.

She had been planning to return on April 23. On April 18, the government barred Hasina from her planned return, saying that she had made provocative statements and that her return could cause disorder. This was described as a temporary measure. Hasina vowed to return home anyway, and on April 22, a warrant was issued by a Bangladeshi court for her arrest. On the same day, Hasina attempted to board a flight back to Bangladesh in London but was not allowed on the flight. Labelling the case against her as "totally false and fake", Hasina said that she wanted to defend herself against the charges in court. On April 23, the arrest warrant was suspended, and on April 25 the ban on Hasina's entry into the country was dropped.

With her rival Khaleda Zia being pressured to go into exile at the same time, the government's actions against Hasina appeared to be an attempt to restructure the political system rather than an attempt to support her rival.

After spending 51 days in the US and UK, at 4:45pm on 7 May 2007 Sheikh Hasina arrived at Zia International Airport in Dhaka, where she was greeted by a jubilant crowd of several thousands. At the airport Hasina told reporters that it was a mistake for the government to stop her from returning and that she hoped it would not "make a bigger mistake", while acknowledging that its reversal was a positive gesture.

JULY 2007 ARREST

On July 16, 2007 Hasina was arrested by state police at her home and taken before a local court in Dhaka. She was accused of extortion and denied bail on the same day, and was held in a building converted into a jail on the premises of the National Parliament. According to the Awami League, the arrest was politically motivated. On July 17, the Anti-Corruption Commission sent a notice to Hasina, along with Zia, requesting that details of her assets be submitted to the Commission within one week.

Hasina's son Sajeeb Wazed Joy stated that the caretaker government was going beyond their limits, saying he did not plan to return to Bangladesh immediately but would try to organize worldwide protest. The arrest was widely seen as move by the military-backed interim government to force Sheikh Hasina from Bangladesh into political exile.Earlier attempts had been made to bar her from coming back to Bangladesh. United Kingdom MPs condemned the arrest.

On July 30, the Dhaka High Court suspended the extortion trial of her and ordered her release on bail. On September 2, an additional case was filed against Hasina by the Anti-Corruption Commission regarding the awarding of a contract for the construction of a power plant in 1997, for which she allegedly took a bribe of 30 million takas and kept the contract from going to the lowest bidder; six others were also accused of involvement. This coincided with a case filed against Zia on the same day.

On January 13, 2008, she was indicted by a special court along with two of her relatives, her sister Sheikh Rehana and her cousin Sheikh Selim, on extortion charges. On February 6, however, the High Court stopped the trial, ruling that she could not be prosecuted under emergency laws for alleged crimes committed prior to the imposition of the state of emergency.

On June 11, 2008 Hasina was released on parole for medical reasons and the next day she flew to the United States to be treated for hearing impairment, eye problems and high blood pressure. Prof. Syed Modasser Ali, her personal physician, threatened to sue the caretaker government over negligence regarding Hasina's treatment during her detention.

ELECTION 2008

November 6, 2008 Hasina returned to Bangladesh to lead her party in general elections scheduled for December 29, 2008. On December 11, 2008 Sheikh Hasina announced her party's election manifesto during a news conference.In her election manifesto she vowed to build a "Digital Bangladesh" by 2021. Sheikh Hasina's Awami league won the elections on 29th December 2008 with an overwhelming majority.

Sheikh Hasina's party defeated Begum Khaleda Zia's BNP in the 2008 Parliamentary Elections. Her party achieved a landslide victory reminiscent to the 1971 elections of Pakistan. Under her leadership, the party has achieved a supermajority in parliament, controlling 230 seats out of 299. She sworn into the office of prime minister for the second time [Prime Minister is the most powerful executive position in Bangladesh, although technically of lower seniority when compared to president] on 6th January, 2009. Begum Zia, however, rejected the results of the election, going as far as to 'thank the Chief Election Commissioner for stage-managing the parliamentary election' she said. But the general election was free, fair and credible according to the views expressed by foreign and local election observers.

PERSONAL LIFE

Sheikh Hasina married M. A. Wazed Mia, a nuclear scientist in 1968 who has passed away on the 9th of May 2009. She has two children - Sajeeb Wazed Joy, and Saima Wazed Hossain Putul. Both of her children live in the United States. Prime Minister Hasina is a member of the Council of Women World Leaders, an International network of current and former women presidents and prime ministers whose mission is to mobilize women leaders globally for collective action on issues of critical importance to women's development.

MARGARET THATCHER

Margaret Hilda Thatcher, Baroness Thatcher LG, OM, PC, FRS (born 13 October 1925) is a retired British politician. She was the Prime Minister of the United Kingdom from 1979 to 1990 and Leader of the Conservative Party from 1975 to 1990. She is the only woman to have held either post.

Born in Grantham in Lincolnshire, England, she went on to read chemistry at Somerville College, Oxford and train as a barrister. She won a seat as an MP from Finchley in 1959, as a Conservative. When Edward Heath formed a government in 1970, he appointed Thatcher as Secretary of State for Education and Science. Four years later, she backed Keith Joseph in his bid to become Conservative party leader, but he was forced to drop out of the election; Thatcher felt that Heath's government had lost direction, so she entered the contest herself and became leader of the Conservative party in 1975. As the Conservative party maintained leads in most polls, Thatcher went on to become Britain's Prime Minister in the 1979 general election.

Thatcher entered 10 Downing Street with a mandate to reverse the UK's economic decline. Her political philosophy and economic policies emphasised reduced state intervention, free markets, entrepreneurialism and the selling off of state owned companies. She gained much support after the 1982 Falklands War and was re-elected the following year. Thatcher took a hard line against trade unions, survived an assassination attempt, and opposed the Soviet Union (her tough-talking rhetoric gained her the nickname the "Iron Lady"); she was re-elected for an unprecedented third term in 1987. The following years would prove difficult, as her Community Charge plan was largely unpopular, and her views regarding the European Community were not shared by others in her Cabinet. She resigned as Prime Minister in November 1990 after Michael Heseltine's challenge to her leadership of the Conservative Party.

Thatcher's tenure as Prime Minister was the longest since that of Lord Salisbury and the longest continuous period in office since Lord Liverpool in the early 19th century. She was the first woman to lead a major political party in the UK, and the first of only three women to hold any of the four great offices of state. She holds a life peerage as Baroness Thatcher, of Kesteven in the County of Lincolnshire, which entitles her to sit in the House of Lords.

EARLY LIFE AND EDUCATION

Margaret Hilda Roberts was born on 13 October 1925 to Alfred Roberts, originally from Northamptonshire, and Beatrice Roberts née Stephenson from Lincolnshire. Thatcher spent her childhood in the town of Grantham in Lincolnshire, where her father owned two grocery shops. She and her older sister Muriel (born 1921, Grantham; died December 2004; married name Cullen) were raised in the flat above the larger of the two located near the railway line. Her father was active in local politics and religion, serving as an Alderman and Methodist lay preacher. He came from a Liberal family but stood as was then customary in local government as an Independent. He lost his post as Alderman in 1952 after the Labour Party won its first majority on Grantham Council in 1950.

Thatcher was brought up a devout Methodist and has remained a Christian throughout her life. After attending Huntingtower Road Primary School, she won a scholarship to Kesteven and Grantham Girls' School. Her school reports show hard work and commitment, but not brilliance. Outside the classroom she played hockey and also enjoyed swimming and walking. Finishing school during the Second World War, she applied for a scholarship to attend Somerville College, Oxford, but was only successful when the winning candidate dropped out. She went to Oxford in 1943 and studied Natural Sciences, specialising in Chemistry. She became President of the Oxford University Conservative Association in 1946, the third woman to hold the post. In 1946 Thatcher took the Final Honour School examination, graduating with a Second Class Bachelor of Arts degree. She subsequently studied crystallography and received a postgraduate BSc degree in 1947. Three years later, in 1950, she achieved a Master of Arts advanced degree, according to her entitlement as an Oxford BA of seven years' standing since matriculation.

Following graduation, Margaret Roberts moved to Colchester in Essex, to work as a research chemist for BX Plastics. During this time she joined the local Conservative Association and attended the party conference at Llandudno in 1948, as a representative of the University Graduate Conservative Association. She was also a member of the Association of Scientific Workers. In January 1949, a friend from Oxford, who was working for the Dartford Conservative Association, told her that they were looking for candidates. After a brief period, she was selected as the Conservative candidate, and she subsequently moved to Dartford, in Kent, to stand for election as a Member of Parliament. To support herself during this period, she went to work for J. Lyons and Co., where she helped develop methods for preserving ice cream and was paid £500 per year.

POLITICAL CAREER BETWEEN 1950 AND 1970

At the 1950 and 1951 elections, she fought the safe Labour seat of Dartford. Although she was unsuccessful in winning the seat losing out to Norman Dodds, she reduced the Labour majority in the constituency by 6,000. She was, at the time, the youngest ever female Conservative candidate and her campaign attracted a higher than normal amount of media attention for a first time candidate. While active in the Conservative Party in Kent, she met Denis Thatcher, whom she married in 1951. Denis was a wealthy divorced businessman who ran his family's firm; he later became an executive in the oil industry. Denis funded his wife's studies for the Bar. She qualified as a barrister in 1953 and specialised in taxation. In the same year her twin children Carol and Mark were born.

Thatcher began to look for a safe Conservative seat in the mid-1950s and was narrowly rejected as candidate for the Orpington by-election in 1955, and was not selected as a candidate in the 1955 election. She had several further rejections before being selected for Finchley in April 1958. She won the seat after hard campaigning during the 1959 election and was elected as a Member of Parliament. Her maiden speech was in support of her Private Member's Bill (Public Bodies (Admission to Meetings) Act 1960) requiring local councils to hold meetings in public, which was successful. In 1961 she went against the Conservative Party's official position by voting for the restoration of birching.

Within two years, in October 1961, she was given a promotion to the front bench as Parliamentary Undersecretary at the Ministry of Pensions and National Insurance. She held this post throughout the administration of Harold Macmillan, until the Conservatives were removed from office in the 1964 election. When Sir Alec Douglas-Home stepped down, Thatcher voted for Edward Heath in the leadership election of 1965 over Reginald Maudling. She was promoted to the position of Conservative spokesman on Housing and Land; in this position, she advocated the Conservative policy of allowing tenants to buy their council houses. The policy would prove to be popular. She moved to the Shadow Treasury team in 1966. As Treasury spokesman, she opposed Labour's mandatory price and income controls, which she argued would produce contrary effects to those intended and distort the economy.

Thatcher established herself as a potent conference speaker at the Conservative Party Conference of 1966, with a strong attack on the high-tax policies of the Labour Government as being steps "not only towards Socialism, but towards Communism". She argued that lower taxes served as an incentive to hard work. Thatcher was one of few Conservative MPs to support Leo Abse's Bill to decriminalise male homosexuality and voted in favour of David Steel's Bill to legalise abortion, as well as a ban on hare coursing. She supported the retention of capital punishment and voted against the relaxation of divorce laws.

In 1967 she was selected by the Embassy of the United States in London to participate in the International Visitor

Leadership Program (then called the Foreign Leader Program), a professional exchange program in which she spent about six weeks visiting various U.S. cities, political figures, and institutions such as the International Monetary Fund. Later that year, Thatcher joined the Shadow Cabinet as Shadow Fuel spokesman. Shortly preceding the 1970 general election, she was promoted to Shadow Transport and, finally, Education.

EDUCATION SECRETARY (1970–1974)

When the Conservative party under Edward Heath won the 1970 general election, Thatcher became Secretary of State for Education and Science. In her first months in office, Thatcher came to public attention as a result of the administration of Edward Heath's decision to cut spending. She gave priority to academic needs in schools, and imposed public expenditure cuts on the state education system, resulting in, against her private protests, the abolition of free milk for school-children aged seven to eleven. She believed that few children would suffer if schools were charged for milk; however she agreed to give younger children a third of a pint, daily, for nutritional purposes. This provoked a storm of protest from the Labour party and the press, and led to the unflattering moniker "Margaret Thatcher, Milk Snatcher". Of the experience, Thatcher later wrote in her autobiography, "I learned a valuable lesson. I had incurred the maximum of political odium for the minimum of political benefit."

She successfully resisted the introduction of library book charges. She did not volunteer spending cuts in her department, contrary to her later beliefs. Her term was marked by support for several proposals for more local education authorities to close grammar schools and to adopt comprehensive secondary education. Thatcher was determined to preserve grammar schools, which prepared more students for admission to universities. She abolished Labour's commitment to comprehensive schooling, and instead left the matter to local education authorities.

LEADER OF THE OPPOSITION (1975–1979)

The Heath government experienced many difficulties between 1970 and 1974. The government executed a series of reversals in its economic policies, dubbed "U-turns". The Conservatives were defeated in the February 1974 general election, and Thatcher's portfolio was changed to Shadow Environment Secretary. In this position she promised to abolish the rating system that paid for local government services, which was a favoured policy proposal within the Conservative Party for many years.

Thatcher agreed that the Heath Government had lost control of monetary policy and had lost direction. After her party lost the second election of 1974 in October, Thatcher, determined to change the direction of the Conservative party, challenged Heath for the Conservative party leadership. She promised a fresh start, and her main support came from the Conservative 1922 Committee.

Unexpectedly, she defeated Heath on the first ballot, and he resigned the leadership. On the second ballot, she defeated Heath's preferred successor, William Whitelaw, and became Conservative Party leader on 11 February 1975. She appointed Whitelaw as her deputy. Heath remained disenchanted with Thatcher to the end of his life for what he, and many of his supporters, perceived as her disloyalty in standing against him.

Thatcher appointed many of Heath's supporters to the Shadow Cabinet, for she had won the leadership as an outsider and then had little power base of her own within the party. Thatcher had to act cautiously to convert the Conservative Party to her monetarist beliefs. She reversed Heath's support for devolved government for Scotland.

On 19 January 1976, she made a speech in Kensington Town Hall in which she made a scathing attack on the Soviet Union. The most famous part of her speech ran:

The Russians are bent on world dominance, and they are rapidly acquiring the means to become the most powerful imperial nation the world has seen. The men in the Soviet Politburo do not have to worry about the ebb and flow of public opinion. They put guns before butter, while we put just about everything before guns.

In response, the Soviet Defence Ministry newspaper Krasnaya Zvezda (Red Star) gave her the nickname "Iron Lady". She took delight in the name and it soon became associated with her image as having an unwavering and steadfast character. She was later nicknamed "Attila the Hen" as well.

The Labour Government was running into difficulties with industrial disputes and rising unemployment, and eventually collapsing public services during the winter of 1978–79, popularly dubbed the "Winter of Discontent". The Conservatives attacked the government's unemployment record, and used advertising hoardings with the slogan "Labour Isn't Working" to assist them. In an interview in January 1978, Thatcher remarked, "people are really rather afraid that this country might be rather swamped by people with a different culture".

Critics regarded the comment as a veiled reference to people of colour, thus pandering to xenophobia and reactionary sentiment. She received 10,000 letters thanking her for raising the subject and the Conservatives gained a lead against Labour in the opinion polls; both parties were at 43% before Thatcher's interview, but the Conservatives took a 48% to 39% lead over Labour immediately after.

In the run up to the 1979 General Election, most opinion polls showed that voters preferred James Callaghan of the Labour party as Prime Minister, even as the Conservative Party maintained a lead in the polls. A fter a successful motion of no confidence in spring 1979, Callaghan's Labour government fell. The Conservatives would go on to win a 44-seat majority in the House of Commons and Margaret Thatcher became the United Kingdom's first female Prime Minister.

PRIME MINISTER (1979–1990)

Thatcher became Prime Minister on 4 May 1979, with a mandate to reverse the UK's economic decline and to reduce the role of the state in the economy. Arriving at 10 Downing Street, she said, in a paraphrase of St. Francis of Assisi:

"Where there is discord, may we bring harmony. Where there is error, may we bring truth. Where there is doubt, may we bring faith. And where there is despair, may we bring hope."

Thatcher was incensed by one contemporary view within the Civil Service, that its job was to manage the UK's decline from the days of Empire, and she wanted the country to assert a higher level of influence and leadership in international affairs. She represented the newly energetic right wing of the Conservative Party and advocated greater independence of the individual from the state and less government intervention. She became a very close ally, philosophically and politically, with President Ronald Reagan, elected in 1980 in the United States. During her tenure as Prime Minister she was said to need just four hours sleep a night.

FIRST GOVERNMENT 1979–1983

Thatcher's political and economic philosophy emphasised reduced state intervention, free markets, and entrepreneurialism.

She vowed to end what she felt was excessive government interference in the economy, and did this through privatising nationally-owned enterprises and selling public housing to tenants. After the James Callaghan Government had concluded that the Keynesian approach to demand-side management failed, Thatcher felt that the economy was not self-righting and that new fiscal judgements had to be made to concentrate on inflation. She began her economic reforms by increasing interest rates to slow the growth of the money supply and thus lower inflation. In accordance with her less-government intervention views, she introduced cash limits on public spending and reduced expenditures on social services such as education (until 1987) and housing. She also placed limits on the printing of money and legal restrictions on trade unions.

GDP and public spending by functional classification	% Change in real terms 1979/80 to 1989/90
GDP	+23.3
Total government spending	+12.9
Law and order	+53.3
Employment and training	+33.3
Health	+31.8
Social security	+31.8
Transport	-5.8
Trade and industry	-38.2
Housing	-67.0
Defence	-3.3

At the time, some Conservatives expressed doubt over Thatcher's policies. Civil unrest in Britain resulted in the British media discussing the need for a policy u-turn. At the 1980 Conservative Party conference, Thatcher addressed the issue directly, saying, "You turn if you want to. The lady's not for turning!"

Thatcher lowered direct taxes on income amid a recession in 1981, but, despite concerns expressed in a letter from 364 leading economists, indirect taxes were increased. In January 1982, the inflation rate had dropped to 8.6% from earlier highs of 18%, and interest rates fell.

By 1983, overall economic growth was stronger and inflation and mortgage rates were at their lowest levels since 1970, though manufacturing output had dropped 30% from 1978 and unemployment reached a figure of 3.6 million.

The term "Thatcherism" came to refer to her policies as well as aspects of her ethical outlook and personal style, including moral absolutism, nationalism, interest in the individual, and an uncompromising approach to achieving political goals. American author Claire Berlinski, who wrote the biography There Is No Alternative: Why Margaret Thatcher Matters argues repeatedly throughout the volume that it was this Thatcherism, specifically her focus on economic reform that set the United Kingdom on the path to recovery and long term growth.

Northern Ireland

In 1981, a number of Provisional IRA and Irish National Liberation Army prisoners in Northern Ireland's Maze Prison went on hunger strike to regain the status of political prisoners, which had been revoked five years earlier under the preceding Labour government. Bobby Sands began the strike, saying that he would fast until death unless prison inmates won concessions over their living conditions. Thatcher refused to countenance a return to political status for the prisoners, famously declaring "Crime is crime is crime; it is not political" and felt that Britain should not negotiate with terrorists. However, despite holding this view in public, the British government made private contact with republican leaders in a bid to bring the hunger strikes to an end. After nine more men had starved to death and the strike had ended, some rights were restored to paramilitary prisoners, but official recognition of political status was not granted. Later that year, Thatcher and Irish Taoiseach Garret FitzGerald established the Anglo-Irish Inter-Governmental Council, which would act as a forum for meetings between the two governments. On 15 November 1985, Thatcher and FitzGerald signed the Hillsborough Anglo-Irish Agreement; the first time a British government gave the Republic of Ireland an advisory role in the governance of Northern Ireland.

The Falklands

On 2 April 1982, a ruling military junta in Argentina invaded the Falkland Islands and South Georgia, a British overseas territory that Argentina had claimed since an 1810s dispute on the British settlement. The following day, Thatcher sent a naval task force to recapture the islands and eject the invaders. The conflict escalated from there, evolving into an amphibious and ground combat operation. Argentina surrendered on 14 June and the operation was deemed a success for the British, despite 258 British casualties. Victory brought a wave of patriotic enthusiasm and support for the government. Thatcher's personal approval rating rose from 30% to 59%, as measured by Mori, and from 29% to 52%, according to Gallup.

Conservative support climbed from 27% to 44%, while Labour's slipped from 34% to 27%.

1983 Election

Economic recovery from the spring of 1982 bolstered the Thatcher government's popularity, and although many contemporary commentators saw the ensuing national poll as a khaki election that was decided by the 'Falklands factor', the war had produced a disaggregated boost to Conservative support of no more than 3% for 3 months, suggesting Thatcher's sustained improvement was due instead to successful macroeconomic management. She also faced a divided opposition: Labour was bitterly split; the party had responded to the New Cold War by moving to the left and adopting a policy of unilateral nuclear disarmament, and had lost many senior leaders to the new Social Democratic Party in alliance with the Liberal Party, preventing the formation of an electoral pact against the Conservatives. Labour leader Michael Foot was a left-winger and generally regarded as unelectable, while Conservatives viewed Thatcher as 'their greatest electoral asset'. In the June 1983 general election, the Conservatives won 42.4% of the vote, the Labour party 27.6% and the Alliance 25.4% of the vote. Although the Conservatives' share of the vote had fallen slightly (1.5%) since 1979, Labour's vote had fallen by far more (9.3%) and under the first past the post system, the Conservatives won a landslide victory with a massive majority. This resulted in the Conservative party having an overall majority of 144 MPs.

SECOND GOVERNMENT 1983–1987

Economic developments

After the 1983 election, the Conservative majority expanded, Thatcher continued to enact her economic policies. The UK government sold most of the large national utilities to private companies. The policy of privatisation, while anathema to many on the Left, was a main component of Thatcherism.

Many people took advantage of share offers, although many sold their shares immediately for a quick profit and therefore the proportion of shares held by individuals rather than institutions did not increase. By the mid 1980s, the number of individual stockholders had tripled, and the UK government had sold 1.5 million publicly owned housing units to their tenants. In 1985, as a deliberate snub, the University of Oxford voted to refuse Thatcher an honorary degree in protest against her cuts in funding for higher education.

Trade unions

Thatcher was committed to reducing the power of the trades unions. Several unions launched strikes in response to legislation introduced to curb their power, but these actions eventually collapsed, and gradually Thatcher's reforms reduced the power and influence of the unions. According to the BBC, Thatcher "managed to destroy the power of the trade unions for almost a generation."

In 1984 the National Union of Mineworkers ordered a strike, without a national ballot, in opposition to proposals to close a large number of mines and cut thousands of jobs. Thatcher refused to meet the demands of the unions and famously referred to the strike, saying, "We had to fight the enemy without in the Falklands. We always have to be aware of the enemy within, which is much more difficult to fight and more dangerous to liberty." Violence was common during the year-long miners' strike; controversial police tactics were used on strikers. Two miners, Dean Hancock and Russell Shankland, were convicted of the murder of a taxi driver and were sentenced to life imprisonment. After a year of striking, in 1985, the NUM leadership conceded without a deal. The Conservative government proceeded to close 25 pits in 1985; by 1992, a total of 97 pits had been closed with the remaining being sold off and privatised in 1994. These actions had great effect on the industrial and political complexion of Great Britain. The closing of the mines resulted in a loss of jobs and thus an increase in unemployment.

In another display of her views of less-government control, Thatcher broke up the state-owned British shipbuilders and privatised the companies. Only few British shipyards survive today.

Brighton bombing

On the early morning of 12 October 1984, the day before her 59th birthday, Thatcher narrowly escaped injury at the Brighton hotel when her hotel was bombed by the Provisional Irish Republican Army. Five people were killed in the attack, including the wife of Cabinet Minister John Wakeham; a prominent member of the Cabinet, Norman Tebbit, was injured, and his wife Margaret was left paralysed. Thatcher was staying at the hotel to attend the Conservative Party Conference, and insisted that the conference open on time the next day. She delivered her speech as planned in defiance of the bombers, a gesture which won widespread approval across the political spectrum, and measurably enhanced her personal popularity with the public.

Cold War

Thatcher took office during the later period of what was known as the Cold War, a period of frosty relations primarily between the Western powers and the communist Soviet Union and its satellites. During her first year as prime minister, Mrs Thatcher supported NATO's decision to deploy US cruise and Pershing missiles in Western Europe. She became very closely aligned with the policies of US President Ronald Reagan (1981–1989), and their closeness produced transatlantic cooperation.

His policy of deterrence against the Soviets contrasted with the policy of détente which the West had pursued during the 1970s, and caused friction with allies who still adhered to the idea of détente. Thatcher permitted US forces to station more than 160 nuclear cruise missiles at Greenham Common, arousing mass protests by the Campaign for Nuclear Disarmament; Thatcher took a hard line against the protestors. She modernised the British naval fleet with Trident II nuclear submarines.

On 19 December 1984, Thatcher and Deng Xiaoping of the People's Republic of China signed the Sino-British Joint Declaration, which committed Hong Kong to the status of a Special Administrative Region. Britain agreed to leave the region in 1997. In April 1986, Thatcher permitted US military forces to utilise British Royal Air Force bases amid the US bombing of Libya. In July 1986, Thatcher expressed her belief that economic sanctions against South Africa would be immoral because they would make thousands of black workers unemployed.

Thatcher was among the first of Western leaders to respond warmly to reformist Soviet leader Mikhail Gorbachev. They met in London in 1984, three months before he became General Secretary. Thatcher declared that she liked him, and told Ronald Reagan, saying, "we can do business together." Following the Reagan-Gorbachev summit meetings from 1985 to 1988, as well as multiple reforms enacted by Gorbachev in the USSR, Thatcher declared in November 1988, "We're not in a Cold War now" but rather in a "new relationship much wider than the Cold War ever was." She continued, "I expect Mr Gorbachev to do everything he can to continue his reforms. We will support it." Thatcher was initially opposed to German reunification, as she worried that a united Germany would align itself closer with the Soviet Union and move away from NATO.

Her liking for defence ties with the United States was demonstrated in the Westland affair when she acted with colleagues to allow the helicopter manufacturer Westland, a vital defence contractor, to refuse to link with the Italian firm Agusta in order for it to link with the management's preferred option, Sikorsky Aircraft Corporation of the United States. Defence Secretary Michael Heseltine, who had pushed the Agusta deal, resigned in protest after this, and remained an influential critic and potential leadership challenger. Thatcher's premiership outlasted the Cold War, which ended in 1989, and those who share her views on it credit her with a part in the West's victory, by both the deterrence and détente postures.

Other domestic issues

In 1986, in a controversial move, the Thatcher government abolished the Greater London Council, and then led by the left-wing Ken Livingstone, as well as six Labour controlled metropolitan county councils.

The government stated that they ordered this to decrease bureaucracy and increase efficiency, and encouraged transferring power to local councils for increased electoral accountability.

Thatcher's opponents, however, held that the move was politically motivated, as the GLC had become a powerful centre of opposition to her government, and the county councils were in favour of higher local government taxes and public spending.

As Prime Minister, Thatcher met weekly with Queen Elizabeth II to discuss government business. She was just six months older than the Queen, and their relationship was one of much scrutiny; though there was never any personal animosity between the two, the consensus was that they did not get along overly well. While they displayed public images that largely contrasted, Tim Bell, a former Thatcher advisor, recalled, "Margaret has the deepest respect for the Queen and all her family". She was said to greet the Queen with a curtsey every time they met.

1987 Election

At the time of the 1987 general election, Labour leader Neil Kinnock presided over a party deeply divided on policy agendas. Margaret Thatcher, in turn, led her party to victory, winning an unprecedented third term with a 102 seat majority, and became the longest continuously serving Prime Minister of the United Kingdom since Lord Liverpool (1812 to 1827), as well as the only Prime Minister of the 20th century to serve three terms. She was elected riding on an economic boom against a weak Labour opposition. The Conservatives won 42.2% of the popular vote, while the Labour party won 30.8% and Alliance won 22.6 %.

THIRD GOVERNMENT 1987–1990

Environmental issues

Thatcher, the former chemist, became publicly concerned with environmental issues in the late 1980s. In 1988, she made a major speech communicating the problems of global warming, ozone depletion and acid rain.

Continuation of economic changes

Thatcher introduced a new system for the government to raise revenue; she replaced local government taxes with a Community Charge or 'Poll tax', in which property tax rates were made uniform, in that the same amount was charged to every individual resident, and the residential property tax was replaced with a head tax whose rate would be established by local governments. Thatcher's revolutionary system was introduced in Scotland in 1989 and in England and Wales the following year.

A sceptical British public was disenchanted with Thatcher's system of local taxation and it was to be among the most unpopular policies of her premiership. What the Thatcher government did not anticipate was that local councils would raise their total shares from the taxes. As a result, the central Government capped rates that seemed out of line, resulting in charges of partisanship and the alienation of small-government Conservatives. The Prime Minister's popularity declined in 1989 as she continued to refuse to compromise on the tax. Unrest mounted and culminated in a number of riots, the most serious of which occurred at Trafalgar Square, London, on 31 March 1990; more than 100,000 protesters attended and more than 400 people were arrested.

A BBC Radio poll in September 1989 indicated that almost three-quarters of the public were also against water privatisation. Despite public opposition to the poll tax and the privatisation of water, electricity, and British Rail, Thatcher remained confident that, as with her other major reforms, the initial public opposition would turn into support after implementation. A MORI poll for the Sunday Times in June 1988 found that more than 60% of voters agreed that in the long term the Thatcher government's policies would improve the state of the economy, while less than 30% disagreed; although income inequality had increased the poor were still better off than in 1979: 74% of Britons said they were satisfied with their present standard of living, while only 18% were dissatisfied.

Europe

At Bruges, Belgium, in 1988, Thatcher made a speech in which she outlined her opposition to proposals from the European Community, a forerunner to the European Union, for a federal structure and increasing centralisation of decision-making. Though she had supported British membership in the EC, Thatcher believed that the role of the organisation should be limited to ensuring free trade and effective competition, and feared that the EC approach to governing was at odds with her views of smaller government and deregulatory trends; in 1988, she remarked, "We have not successfully rolled back the frontiers of the state in Britain, only to see them re-imposed at a European level, with a European super-state exercising a new dominance from Brussels". A split was emerging over European policy inside the British Government and her Conservative Party.

On 30 November 1988, when the European Court of Human Rights ruled that Britain's detention provisions were in breach of European law, the policy split extended to parliament with the presentation of a petition calling for a written British constitution. Thatcher reacted angrily to the ECHR ruling, and to the failure of Belgium and Ireland to extradite a suspected terrorist, Father Patrick Ryan, to face charges in Britain. She told the Commons: "We shall consider the judgment carefully and also the human rights of the victims and potential victims of terrorism."

At a meeting before the Madrid European Community summit in June 1989, Chancellor of the Exchequer Nigel

Lawson and Foreign Secretary Geoffrey Howe sought to persuade Thatcher to agree to circumstances under which Great Britain would join the Exchange Rate Mechanism, a preparation for monetary union, and abolish the pound sterling as British currency. At the meeting, they both said they would resign if their demands were not met. Thatcher, as well as her economic advisor Alan Walters, was opposed to this notion and felt that the pound sterling should be able to float freely, and that membership would constrain the UK economy. Both Lawson and Howe eventually resigned and Thatcher remained firmly opposed to British membership in the European Monetary System.

1989 Leadership election

Thatcher was challenged for the leadership of the Conservative Party by virtually unknown backbench MP Sir Anthony Meyer in the 1989 leadership election. Of the 374 Conservative MPs eligible to vote, 314 voted for Thatcher while 33 voted for Meyer; there were 27 abstentions. Thatcher noted, "I would like to say how very pleased I am with this result and how very pleased I am to have had the overwhelming support of my colleagues in the House and the people from the party in the country", while Meyer said he was delighted as well: "The total result I think is rather better than I had expected". Her supporters in the Party viewed the results as a success, and rejected suggestions that there was discontent within the Party.

Gulf War

Thatcher was visiting the United States when she received word that Iraqi leader Saddam Hussein had invaded neighbouring Kuwait. She met with US President George H. W. Bush, who had succeeded Ronald Reagan in 1989, during which Bush asked her, "Margaret, what is your view?" She recalled in an interview that she felt "that aggressors must be stopped, not only stopped, but they must be thrown out. An aggressor cannot gain from his aggression. He must be thrown out and really, by that time in my mind, I thought we ought to throw him out so decisively that he could never think of doing it again." She put pressure on Bush to deploy troops to the Middle East to drive the Iraqi army out of Kuwait. Bush was somewhat apprehensive about the plan, so Thatcher remarked to him during a telephone conversation, "This was no time to go wobbly!" Thatcher's government provided military forces to the international coalition in the Gulf War to pursue the ouster of Iraq from Kuwait.

Resignation

Despite having the longest continuous period of office of any prime minister in the twentieth century, Thatcher had, on average during her premiership, the second-lowest approval rating of any post-war prime minister, at 40%, only beating Edward Heath; even after the Falklands War it had never risen above 55%; polls consistently showed that she was less popular than the Conservative party. A self-described conviction politician, Thatcher always insisted she did not care about her poll ratings, pointing instead to her unbeaten election record.

Moreover, in relative terms, Thatcher's personal position had remained consistently strong: a Marplan poll for the Sunday Express in October 1988 showed that Thatcher was still trusted by 61% of Britons to lead the country, compared with only 17% for Labour leader Neil Kinnock. Thatcher's capacity to lead was trusted by 87% of Conservative voters and 46% of Labour voters. A Telephone Surveys poll for the Sunday Express in September 1990, during the Gulf crisis, found that 65% of voters preferred Thatcher as a crisis leader to Kinnock, who polled 20%.

A Mori poll for the Sunday Times in September 1989 showed that Thatcher was still the public's preferred choice of Conservative leader, attracting the support of 32% of voters, her pro-European former cabinet colleague Michael Heseltine coming second on 22%. However, by March 1990, in the face of high inflation and rising unemployment, Thatcher's support had halved to 15%, with Heseltine's doubling to 40%. Opposition to the poll tax and the divisions opening in the parliamentary party over European integration left Thatcher increasingly vulnerable to a challenge.

By November 1990 the Conservatives had been trailing Labour for 18 months. Although a Mori survey for the Sunday Times showed that 83% of Conservative voters were satisfied by the way Thatcher represented the United Kingdom in Europe, a BBC poll found that Labour had increased its lead by 5 points to 14%, its biggest lead since May, while a poll for the Evening Standard found that Labour had nearly doubled its lead over the Conservatives to 13.2 points. Low poll ratings, along with Thatcher combative personality and willingness to override colleagues' opinions, contributed to discontent in the parliamentary party.

On 1 November 1990, Geoffrey Howe, for 15 years one of Thatcher's most 'loyal and self-effacing' supporters, resigned from his position as Deputy Prime Minister over her refusal to agree to a timetable for British membership of the single currency. In his resignation speech in the Commons on 13 November, referring to Thatcher's promise to veto any arrangement which jeopardised the pound sterling, Howe famously complained: 'It is rather like sending your opening batsmen to the crease only for them to find the moment that the first balls are bowled that their bats have been broken before the game by the team captain.' Howe's resignation put Thatcher's future in doubt, and was afterwards recognised as dealing a 'fatal blow' to her premiership. While 59% of the British public polled for The Independent by Number Market Research agreed with Thatcher's opposition to monetary union, 64% still felt she ought to retire.

A few days later Heseltine challenged her for the leadership of the party. A Gallup poll for the Daily Telegraph showed that 28% of voters would be more inclined to vote Conservative if Heseltine were leader, and only 7% would be less inclined. Five separate polls indicated that he would give the Conservatives a national lead over Labour. Heseltine attracted sufficient support from the parliamentary party in the first round of voting to prolong the contest to a second ballot. Although Thatcher initially stated that she intended to contest the second ballot, she consulted with her Cabinet and decided to withdraw from the contest. Thatcher said that pressure from her colleagues helped her to conclude that the unity of the Conservative Party and the prospect of victory in the next general election would be more likely if she resigned. On 22 November, at 09.34, the 65 year old Prime Minister announced to the Cabinet that she would not be a candidate in the second ballot. A statement was soon released from 10 Downing Street:

"The Prime Minister, the Rt. Hon. Margaret Thatcher, F.R.S., has informed the Queen that she does not intend to contest the second ballot of the election for leadership of the Conservative Party and intends to resign as Prime Minister as soon as a new leader of the Conservative Party has been elected... Having consulted widely among my colleagues, I have concluded that the unity of the Party and the prospects of victory in a General Election would be better served if I stood down to enable Cabinet colleagues to enter the ballot for the leadership. I should like to thank all those in Cabinet and outside who have given me such dedicated support."

Some sections of the British public were stunned, but there were also scenes of rejoicing at the news. Thatcher went to Buckingham Palace to inform the Queen of her decision. She later arrived at the House of Commons to a debate; Neil Kinnock, Leader of the Opposition, proposed a motion of no confidence in the government, and Thatcher displayed her combativeness. She said:

"Eleven years ago we rescued Britain from the parlous state to which socialism had brought it. Once again Britain stands tall in the councils of Europe and of the world. Over the last decade, we have given power back to the people on an unprecedented scale. We have given back control to people over their own lives and over their livelihoods, over the decisions that matter most to them and their families. We have done it by curbing the monopoly power of trade unions to control, even victimize the individual worker."

LATER YEARS

Mrs Thatcher retained her parliamentary seat in the House of Commons as MP for Finchley for two years despite returning to the backbenches after leaving the premiership. She supported John Major as her successor and he duly won the leadership contest, although in the years to come her approval of Major would fall away. She occasionally spoke in the House of Commons after she was Prime Minister, commenting and campaigning on issues regarding her beliefs and concerns. In 1991, she was given a five minute, unprecedented standing ovation at the party's annual conference. She retired from the House at the 1992 election, at the age of 66 years; she said that leaving the Commons would allow her more freedom to speak her mind.

AFTER PARLIAMENT

Margaret Thatcher became a peer in House of Lords in 1992 by the bestowal of a life peerage as Baroness Thatcher, of Kesteven in the County of Lincolnshire. Thatcher had already been honoured by the Queen in 1990, shortly after her resignation as Prime Minister, when awarded the Order of Merit, one of the UK's highest distinctions and in the personal conferment of the sovereign. At the same time it was announced that her husband, Denis, would be given a baronetcy, which was confirmed in 1991 (ensuring that their son, Mark, would inherit a title). In 1995, Baroness Thatcher was appointed a Lady Companion of the Order of the Garter, the United Kingdom's highest order of Chivalry.

After leaving the House of Commons, Thatcher remained active in politics. She authored her memoirs in two volumes: The Path to Power and The Downing Street Years, the former released in 1995 and the latter two years prior. She later published a third book, Statecraft: Strategies for a Changing World, detailing her thoughts on international relations since her resignation in 1990. The chapters on the European Union were particularly controversial; she called for a fundamental renegotiation of Britain's membership to preserve the UK's sovereignty and, if that failed, for Britain to leave and join NAFTA.

In August 1992 Thatcher called for NATO to stop the Serbian assault on Goražde and Sarajevo in order to end ethnic cleansing and to preserve the Bosnian state. She described the situation in Bosnia as "reminiscent of the worst excesses of the Nazis," warning that there could be a "holocaust" in Bosnia and described the conflict as a "killing field the like of which I thought we would never see in Europe again." She made a series of speeches in the Lords criticising the Maastricht Treaty, describing it as "a treaty too far" and stated "I could never have signed this treaty". She cited A. V. Dicey, to the effect that, since all three main parties were in favour of revisiting the treaty, the people should have their say.

From 1993 to 2000, Lady Thatcher served as Chancellor of the College of William and Mary in Virginia, which, established by Royal Charter in 1693, is the sole royal foundation in the contiguous United States. She was also Chancellor of the University of Buckingham, the UK's only private university.

After Tony Blair's election as Labour Party leader in 1994, Thatcher gave an interview in May 1995 in which she praised Blair as "probably the most formidable Labour leader since Hugh Gaitskell. I see a lot of socialism behind their front bench, but not in Mr Blair. I think he genuinely has moved."

Lady Thatcher visited former Chilean president Augusto Pinochet, once a key British ally during the 1982 Falklands War, while he was under house arrest in Surrey in 1998. Pinochet was fighting extradition to Spain for alleged human rights abuses committed during his tenure. Thatcher expressed her support and friendship for Pinochet, thanking him for his support in 1982 and for "bringing democracy to Chile."

In 1999, during Thatcher's first speech to a Conservative Party conference in nine years, she contended that Britain's problems came from continental Europe. Her comments aroused some criticism from Sir Malcolm Rifkind, a former

Foreign Secretary under Sir John Major, who said that Lady Thatcher's comments could give the impression that Britain is prejudiced against Europe.

In the 2001 general election, Lady Thatcher supported the Conservative general election campaign but this time did not endorse Iain Duncan Smith in public as she had done previously for John Major and William Hague. In the Conservative leadership election shortly after, she supported Iain Duncan Smith because she believed he would "make infinitely the better leader" than Kenneth Clarke.

ACTIVITIES SINCE 2003

Thatcher was widowed upon the death of Sir Denis Thatcher on 26 June 2003. A funeral service was held honouring him at the Royal Hospital in Chelsea on 3 July with Thatcher present, as well as her children Mark and Carol. Thatcher paid tribute to him by saying, "Being Prime Minister is a lonely job. In a sense, it ought to be you cannot lead from a crowd. But with Denis there I was never alone. What a man. What a husband. What a friend".

The following year, on 11 June, Thatcher travelled to the United States to attend the state funeral service for former US President Ronald Reagan and one of her closest friends at the National Cathedral in Washington, D.C. Thatcher delivered a eulogy via videotape to Reagan; in view of her failing mental faculties following several small strokes, the message had been pre-recorded several months earlier. Thatcher then flew to California with the Reagan entourage, and attended the memorial service and interment ceremony for President Reagan at the Ronald Reagan Presidential Library.

Thatcher marked her 80th birthday with a celebration at the Mandarin Oriental Hotel in Hyde Park on 13 October 2005, where the guests included the Queen, The Duke of Edinburgh, Princess Alexandra and Tony Blair. There, Geoffrey Howe, now Lord Howe of Aberavon, said of his former boss, "Her real triumph was to have transformed not just one party but two, so that when Labour did eventually return, the great bulk of Thatcherism was accepted as irreversible."

In 2006, Thatcher attended the official Washington, D.C. memorial service to commemorate the fifth anniversary of the 11 September 2001 attacks on the United States. She attended as a guest of the US Vice President, Dick Cheney, and met with US Secretary of State Condoleezza Rice during her visit. On 12 November, she appeared at the Remembrance Day parade at the Cenotaph in London, leaning heavily on the arm of Sir John Major. On 10 December she announced she was "deeply saddened" by the death of Augusto Pinochet.

In February 2007, she became the first Prime Minister of the United Kingdom to be honoured with a statue in the Houses of Parliament while still living. The statue is made of bronze and stands opposite her political hero and predecessor, Sir Winston Churchill. The statue was unveiled on 21 February 2007 with Lady Thatcher in attendance; she made a rare and brief speech in the members' lobby of the House of Commons, reposting, "I might have preferred iron - but bronze will do... It won't rust." The statue shows her as if she were addressing the House of Commons, with her right arm outstretched. Thatcher said she was thrilled with it.

On 13 September 2007, Thatcher was invited to 10 Downing Street to have tea with Prime Minister Gordon Brown and his wife, Sarah. Brown referred to Lady Thatcher as a "conviction politician" and said of him, "I'm a conviction politician just like her." William Hague attacked this decision, saying to Brown, "You may fawn now at the feet of our greatest prime minister – but you are no Margaret Thatcher. Margaret Thatcher would never have devastated the pension funds of this nation, nor kicked its small businesses in the teeth. We, Gordon, backed her when she rescued our country in the face of every denunciation and insult from the likes of you. Brown's spokesman insisted that the meeting was "not unusual", that it was customary for Prime Ministers to invite their predecessors to tea and that Mr Brown would be "happy" to meet any former Prime Minister.

On 30 January 2008, Thatcher met incumbent Conservative Leader David Cameron at an awards ceremony at London's Guildhall where she was presented with a 'Lifetime Achievement Award'.

HEALTH CONCERNS

Thatcher suffered several small strokes in 2002 and she was advised by her doctors not to engage in any more public speaking. As a result of the strokes, her short term memory began to falter. Her former press spokesman Sir Bernard Ingham said in early 2007, "She's now got no short-term memory left, which is absolutely tragic."

Thatcher was admitted to St Thomas' Hospital, Central London on 7 March 2008, for tests after collapsing at a House of Lords dinner. She was taken by ambulance to the hospital, where she spent one night. The incident was probably caused by her low blood pressure and stuffy conditions within the dining hall.

On 24 August 2008 it was publicly disclosed that Thatcher has been suffering from dementia. Her daughter Carol described in her 2008 memoir, A Swim-on Part in the Goldfish Bowl, first observing in 2000 that Thatcher was becoming forgetful. The condition later became more noticeable; at times, Thatcher thought that her husband Denis, who died in 2003, was still living. Carol Thatcher recalls that her mother's memories of the time she spent as Prime Minister from 1979 to 1990 remain among her sharpest.

LEGACY

Thatcher is well remembered for her famed remarks to the reporter Douglas Keay, for *Woman's Own* magazine, 23 September 1987:

I think we have gone through a period when too many children and people have been given to understand "I have a problem, it is the Government's job to cope with it!" or "I have a problem, I will go and get a grant to cope with it!" "I am homeless, the Government must house me!" and so they are casting their problems on society and who is society? There is no such thing! There are individual men and women and there are families and no government can do anything except through people and people look to themselves first. It is our duty to look after ourselves and then also to help look after our neighbour and life is a reciprocal business and people have got the entitlements too much in mind without the obligations...

To her supporters, Margaret Thatcher remains a revolutionary figure who revitalised Britain's economy, impacted the trade unions, and re-established the nation as a world power. She contributed greatly to the end of the Cold War and the fall of communism. But Thatcher was also a controversial figure, in that her premiership was also marked by high unemployment and social unrest. Many critics fault her economic policies for the unemployment level. Speaking in Scotland in April 2009, before the 30th anniversary of her election as prime minister, Thatcher declared: 'I regret nothing,' and insisted 'she was right to introduce the poll tax and to close loss-making industries to end the country's "dependency culture".'

The Labour party, in modernising its social democratic agenda to make itself electable and 'market friendly', incorporated much of the economic, social and political tenets of Thatcherism. Thatcher's programme of privatising state-owned enterprises has not been reversed. Indeed, successive Conservative and Labour governments have further curtailed the involvement of the state in the economy and have further dismantled public ownership.

After her resignation in 1990, a MORI poll found that 52% of Britons agreed that "On balance she had been good for the country", while 48% disagreed, thinking she had not. In April 2008, the Daily Telegraph commissioned a YouGov poll asking whom Britons regarded as the greatest post-World War II prime minister; Thatcher came in first, receiving 34% of the vote, while Winston Churchill ranked second with 15%. Thatcher has been the subject of a number of television programs, documentaries, films and plays; among the most notable depictions of her are Patricia Hodge in The Falklands Play (1986) and Lindsay Duncan in Margaret (2009). She was also the inspiration for a number of protest songs.

Recently proponents of the 'end of capitalism' thesis have speculated tentatively about 'the death of Thatcherism', linking the 1986 deregulation of the financial industry to the 2008 world financial crisis. The Economist, however, rejected a link, countering: 'There have been too many intervening years, factors and governments for the case to stand up though it reflects Mrs Thatcher's mythic status that, for some, she must be to blame.'

Conversely, Conservative leaders sense in crisis 'the death of New Labour'. Thatcher's defenders argue that the current downturn is dwarfed by the wealth generated by decades of growth, and note that the banking crisis began under the divided, tripartite regulatory system introduced by Gordon Brown in 1997. Others point to Thatcher's control of the money supply and cite the 1986 Financial Services Act as evidence of her own emphasis on 'stringent banking regulation', and contend that the big-spending Labour government only lasted as long as it did 'because it inherited the best economic situation of any 20th-century government'.

Thatcher herself made known in April 2009 that she was 'appalled' by Brown's handling of the economy, seeing it as 'a repeat' of the crisis of the 1970s that had brought her radical reforming government to power. Pointing to the 'huge convergence around liberal labour markets, liberal migration policies and high levels of public spending,' one leading analyst summed up the new policy paradigm as: 'Thatcher plus Keynes.'

HONOURS

In addition to her conventional appointment as a Member of Her Majesty's Most Honourable Privy Council (PC) upon becoming Secretary of State for Education and Science in 1970 Thatcher has received numerous honours as a result of her career, including being named a Lady of the Most Noble Order of the Garter (LG). She is a Member of the Order of Merit (OM) as well as a Fellow of the Royal Society (FRS) and the first woman entitled to full membership rights as an honorary member of the Carlton Club, a gentlemen's club.

In 1999 Thatcher was among 18 included in Gallup's List of Widely Admired People of the 20th century, from a poll conducted of Americans. In a 2006 list compiled by New Statesman, she was voted 5th in the list of "Heroes of our time". She was also named a "Hero of Freedom" by the libertarian magazine Reason. In the Falkland Islands, Margaret Thatcher Day is celebrated as a public holiday every 10 January, commemorating her visit on this date in 1983, seven months after the military victory; the decision was taken by the Falklands Islands legislature in 1992. Thatcher Drive in Stanley, the site of government, is also named for her. In South Georgia, Thatcher Peninsula, where the Task Force troops first set foot on Falkland's soil, also bears her name.

Upon her death, it has been suggested that Lady Thatcher be granted the rare honour of a state funeral. However, this has proved controversial, and the government has stated that they are undecided on the issue.

Thatcher has also been awarded numerous honours from foreign countries. In 1990, she was awarded the Presidential Medal of Freedom, the highest civilian honour awarded by the United States. She was also given the Republican Senatorial Medal of Freedom, Ronald Reagan Freedom Award, and named a patron of the Heritage Foundation. She was also awarded the Grand Order of King Dmitar Zvonimir, the highest state order of the Republic of Croatia.

Margaret Thatcher's arms. The admiral represents the Falklands War, the image of Sir Isaac Newton her background as a chemist and her birth town Grantham.

Bibliography

Addams Jane, Emily Balch, and Alice Hamilton. *Women at The Hague*. New York : n.p., 1915.

Arnold Bruce, *A Study in Power (Thatcher)*. London: Hamilton,1984.

Baxter Sandra, and Marjorie Lansing. *Women and Politics. The Invisible Majority*. Ann Arbor: University of Michigan Press, 1980.

Bhutto Benazir. *Daughter of Destiny: An Autobiograpby*. New York: Simon & Schus- ter, 1989.

Blake Robert. *The Conservative Party from Peel to Thatcher*. London: Methuen, 1985.

Boserup Ester. *Women's Role in Economic Development*. New York: St. Martin's, 1970.

Boulding Elise. *Women: The Fifth World*. New York: Foreign Policy Association, 1980.

Bulbeck Chilla. *One World Women's Movement*. London: Pluto, 1988.

Bunch Charlotte, and Roxanna Carrillo. "Feminist Perspectives on Women in Development." *In Persistent Inequalities. Women and World Development*, ed. Irene Tinker. New York: Oxford University Press, 1990.

Bandarage, Asoka. "Women in Development: Liberalism, Marxism and Marxist Feminist." *Development and Change* 15 (495-515, 1984).

Banderage, Asoka. "Third World Women: More than Mere Statistics." *Women's Review of Books* (November 1983).

Brown, Wendy. *Manhood and Politics*. Totowa, NJ: Rowman and Littlefield, 1988.

Connell, R.W. "The State, Gender and Sexual Politics: Theory and Appraisal." *Theory and Society* (1990).

Conway, Jill K., Susan C. Bourque, and Joan W. Scott. *Learning About Women: Gender, Politics & Power*. Ann Arbo: University of Michigan Press, 1987.

D'Amico, francine and Peter Beckman, eds. *Women and World Politics*. forthcoming.

Di Stefano, Christine. *Configurations of Masculinity: A Feminist Perspective on Modern Political Theory*. Ithaca and London: Cornell University Press, 1991.

Eisenstein, Hester. *Contemporary Feminist Thought*. Boston: G.K. Hall, 1983.

Eisenstein, Hester and Alice Jardine, ed. *The Future of Difference*. Boston: G.K. Hall & Co., 1980.

Fuss, Diana. *Essentially Speaking: Feminism, Nature and Differrence*. New York: Routledge, 1989.

Gailey, Christine Ward. "Women and Warfare: Shifting Status in Precapitalist State Formation." *Culture* 4 (61-70 1984).

Haraway, Donna. "Situated Knowledges." *Feminist Studies* 14 (3 (Fall) 1988).

Hekman, Susan J. *Gender and Knowledge: Elements of a Postmodern Feminism*. Cambridge: Polity Press, 1990.

Jaggar, Alison. *Feminist Politics and Human Nature*. Totowa, NJ: Rowman and Allanheld, 1983.

Jayawardena, Kumari. *Feminism and Nationalism in the Third World*. London: ZED Books, 1986.

Lips, Hilary. *Women, Men, and Power*. Mountain View, CA: Mayfield, 1991.

Nash, June and Fernandez-Kelly, ed. *Women, Men, and the International Division of Labor*. Albany: State University of New York Press, 1983.

Nations, United. *The World's Women: 1970-1990 Trends and Statistics.*United Nations, 1991.

Okin, Susan Moller. *Women in Western Political Thought.* Princeton, NJ: Princeton University Press, 1979.

Pateman, Carole. *The Problem of Political Obligation.* Berkeley: University of California Press, 1985.

Randall, Vicky. *Women and Politics: An International Perspective.* Chicago: University of Chicago Press, 1987.

Reynolds, Sian, ed. *Women, State and Revolution: Essays on Power and Gender in Europe Since 1789.* Wheatsheaf Books, 1986.

Rowbotham, Sheila. *Women, Resistance and Revolution: A History of Women and Revolution in the Modern World.* New York: Vintage Books, 1974.

Ruddick, Sara. *Maternal Thinking: Toward a Politics of Peace.* Boston: Beacon Press, 1989.

Staudt, Kathleen, ed. *Women, International Development, and Politics: The BureaucraticQuagmire.* Philadelphia: Temple University Press, 1990.

Staudt, Kathleen and Jane Jaquette. *Women in Developing Countries: A Policy Focus.* New York: Hayworth Press, 1983.

Tong, Rosemarie. *Feminist Thought.* Boulder, Co: Westview, 1989.

University, Oxford. *Women: A World Report.* Oxford University Press, 1985.

Walker, Cheryl. *Women in Southern Africa: A Bibiography.* Durban: University of Natal; Durban Women's Bibliography Group, 1985.

Ward, Kathryn B. *Women in the World System: Its Impact on Status and Fertility.* New York: Praeger, 1984.

Yuval-Davis, Nira and Floya Antias, ed. *Woman-Nation-State.* London: Macmillan Press, 1989.

INDEX

Index